Lord, Have Mercy

Discovering Jesus in the Days Before Easter
A Family Devotional Guide for Lent

Amy M. Edwards

ISBN-13: 978-1494931582
ISBN-10: 1494931583

This book is dedicated to my husband,
Howard Edwards.
May God grant us grace that we might be able to proclaim
Christ to our children.

✝

For Hope, Sydney, Lane, Tobias, and Lydia,
who inspired me to write this devotional.
May you feast on the Bread of Life all of your lives.

✝

AME

CONTENTS

Preface

Gathering your family for regular family devotions is a challenge and few families are able to consistently gather around for devotions every day of the week. Relax. Any time that you spend together in the Word of God is valuable. While this book provides devotions for Mondays through Saturdays in the weeks of Lent (forty days before Easter), feel free to use the devotions in this book however you like, anytime of year. It may take forty days, or you may take forty weeks, but your time as a family in God's Word will be worth it.

Perhaps you are only able to gather a few times a week, but you want to progress through each week of Lent leading up to the crucifixion and resurrection. Select a few devotions from each week and skip the others.

Perhaps you'd like to use all the devotions, but aren't able to keep up with an everyday routine. Don't worry. The devotions in this book are taken from the ministry of Jesus. While they are scheduled for Lent, your family can meditate on Jesus and the Gospel any week of the year.

If you find that each devotional session takes longer than your family has to spend together, feel free to shorten your discussion by leaving out some questions. If your children are older, you may find it better to skip the initial questions. On the other hand, if your children are younger, you may decide to skip some of the deeper thinking questions.

For more information on using this devotion to lead your family in meditating on the Scriptures, refer to the Introduction that follows.

INTRODUCTION

Family devotions can help us make Easter what it should be, the Christian's most treasured holiday.

Our family life is full of tradition in the weeks of Advent, leading up to Christmas. But as much as we love Christmas, something seems out of balance when Easter doesn't have the same attention and spiritual focus as Christmas. To be sure, the Incarnation that we glory in at Christmas time is a miracle worthy of celebration, but even this miracle is empty without the promise of a coming Good Friday and Easter.

THE TRADITION OF LENT

Having grown up in an evangelical church that didn't observe the historic church calendar, I didn't know much about Lent as a child and teen. Ash Wednesday and Lent were foreign traditions to me, just as were liturgy and prayer books.

Apart from Christmas and Easter, the church calendar and its traditions were not embraced by non-mainline denominations in the

20th century. Liturgy had come to be associated with rote and meaningless church services. The written prayers, scheduled traditions, and observance of holy days that were meant to keep people strong in their faith seemed to fail in their purpose. Liturgies rich with doctrine and spiritual truth were recited by many churchgoers without conviction in their hearts, and some evangelicals reacted by worshipping together in a very different way.

History of Lent

The word "Lent" comes into English from an Anglo-Saxon word for "spring," *lencten*. In early church history, Christians began fasting to prepare their hearts for Easter. Over time, the Church settled on a forty day fasting period, echoing Jesus's forty days and nights of fasting in the desert. In the Old Testament, the rains fell on the earth forty days and nights while Noah and his family were saved in the ark (Gen. 7:12). Moses spent forty days and nights on Mount Sinai, communing with the LORD and fasting from bread and water (Ex. 24:18). Elijah made a special forty-days-and-nights journey to Mount Horeb (Sinai), the Mount of God, without partaking of food on the way. The choice of forty days to fast seems to have a good biblical foundation.

The Church developed rules for the Lenten fast, although apparently these rules varied over time and by area. Pope Gregory the Great (c. 540-604) moved the first day of Lent to Wednesday. Christians were required to mark the first day of the fast by coming to the church to repent of their sins. They received a mark of a cross, made with ashes, on their foreheads as a visible mark of their grief for their sin. They followed Ash Wednesday with forty days of fasting. They didn't go entirely without food, but instead the Church gave its people specific rules about foods that were legal and those that were illegal during the time of fasting.

From the days of Abraham God has given us tangible illustrations of spiritual truths. Circumcision. Blood on the doorposts. The Law and Tabernacle. Sacrifices. Dietary laws. It makes sense that the Church would develop traditions as living metaphors meant to shed light on spiritual abstractions, especially at a time when few people were able to read and few copies of the Bible were accessible for those who could read. *Lenten fasting was a commandment of men, however, held as a doctrine of God.* Jesus had a warning about such things. "You hypocrites! Well did Isaiah prophesy of you, when he said: 'This people honors me with their lips, but their heart is far from me; in vain do they worship me, teaching as doctrines the commandments of men.'" (Matthew 15:7-8)

Nine hundred years after Pope Gregory, John Calvin had little use for Lenten fasting and its accompanying Church requirements. In his *Institutes* he called Lent a "superstitious observance." Calvin took issue with Lenten fasting as an imitation of Christ's desert fast saying, "Christ did not fast repeatedly (which he must have done had he meant to lay down a law for an anniversary fast), but once only, when preparing for the promulgation of the gospel." Calvin warned that spiritual disciplines like fasting became superstitious when people did them for the approval of others, not God. As it says in Joel 2: 12-13a, "Yet even now," declares the LORD, "return to me with all your heart, with fasting, with weeping, and with mourning; and rend your hearts and not your garments."

Embracing the Tradition in an Evangelical Way

The LORD tells us to rend our hearts, not our garments, in repentance to Him. Like church bishops of the past, I wish I could institute rules and practices for my children to follow that would secure their faith and assure me that they will respond to Christ in repentance. The problem is that I cannot rend my child's heart for them anymore than I can be their Savior. True repentance is different from, yet one with, regeneration. It is the work of the Holy Spirit.

As a parent, I can set an example of repentant fasting, but if I require it of my children, I'm creating what Calvin called a superstition. This will never do. Can there be any value, then, in observing Lent in our homes?

Lent, Easter, and the Gospel

My prayer is that this book of family devotions will help your family prepare for a glorious Easter and help you succeed in bringing your family together in the Word. Rather than observing Lent as a set of rules and regulations, let's make it a time to fix our eyes on Jesus. Lent should be Christ-centered, not me-centered. What a wonderful opportunity Lent gives us to focus on Jesus and His earthly ministry and the meaning of the Gospel.

It isn't easy to maintain a family devotional habit. Evening activities rush us, leaving little time to gather. Differences in the ages of our children make it difficult to keep everyone engaged in what we are reading. Inevitably, at least one of the kids tunes out. Worst of all, sometimes our kids complain about our attempts to have devotions. Devotions are a time devoted to worship, Scripture, and prayer. These things are not always entertaining, and some kids lose patience and complain of boredom. For parents who yearn for their kids to know and love God, this is crushing. May this devotional help you overcome these challenges.

When is Lent?

Lent is calculated as the forty days before Easter, excluding Sundays, which, as the Lord's Day, were days for breaking the fast with a feast. This makes the period of Lent six and a half weeks long.

Here are dates for Ash Wednesday, the first day of Lent, and Easter for the next ten years, following the Western church calendar:

2014: March 5; April 20
2015: February 18; April 5
2016: February 10; March 27
2017: March 1; April 16
2018: February 14; April 1
2019: March 6; April 21
2020: February 26; April 12

2021: February 17; April 4
2022: March 2; April 17
2023: February 22; April 9

HOW TO USE THIS DEVOTIONAL: FOUR EASY STEPS

This book provides you with a daily devotion for every day during Lent, the forty days preceding Easter, excluding Sundays. Begin on Ash Wednesday (check the date from the list above). Should you get a late start, don't worry, just begin on the current day's devotion. Don't feel that you must catch up. Each week's devotions cover a different aspect of Christ's ministry. While you will be blessed by God's Word if you can do it daily, you won't miss the main point of the week if you miss a day or two. If you can't complete the day's devotion, do as much as you can in the time that you have, shortening discussion by reading provided answers aloud. We often have our devotional time after our evening meal. Sometimes we take 15 minutes, sometimes 30.

Collect your family together and give everyone a Bible. Even pre-readers will enjoy holding their own Bible. You can open with a simple prayer such as, "Lord, quiet our hearts and open our eyes to Your instruction."

Step One: Reading the Scripture

A good family devotional needs to be centered on the Word of God. Each daily devotion in this book begins with a reading from the Bible. We often have our older kids take turns reading the selection. Sometimes we all have our Bibles open and each of us reads a verse or two. Other times my husband will call on one of us to read the full selection, or sometimes he reads it to us.

Step Two: Discussion Questions

Following the Scripture reading, questions are given for you to read to your family. Discussion questions are written to encourage a dialogue that moves from concrete observations (so helpful and important for your younger kids) to abstract truths (so essential to understanding Christ for your older kids). Address the easy and straight-forward questions to your youngest children and challenge your older kids with the more difficult thinking questions. If you don't have kids old enough for the thinking questions, go through them anyway with your spouse. It is a beautiful thing for even your youngest children to see you talking about God's Word.

Step Three: Discussion

Possible answers are given in italics to make it easy for you to guide your family into discovering truths about the Scripture passage. You do not need to read the italicized answers exactly, but can refer to them as you shepherd your family toward understanding the passage. If children answer questions differently from what is written in italics, do not tell them they are wrong. Listen, praise, and encourage your kids as they give various answers to the thinking questions. If their thoughts don't match up to the italicized answers, that's okay. Read the provided answer by saying, "A better answer is..." or, "Another way to think about this is..." If you are pressed for time, simply read the answers rather than wait for discussion.

Together your family will converse about the Scriptures. By God's grace your eyes will be opened to the wonders of God's mercy that are given to us in Jesus Christ.

Step Four: Prayer

A sample closing prayer is provided to help you lead your family in prayer. You may read it as a prayer and then add your own prayer, or use the sample to say something like it in your own words.

✝

I pray that you and your family will grow in knowing Jesus as much or more than I have as I've written these devotions. We need His mercy and He is so faithful to give it to us in Christ. May the centuries-old liturgy be our prayer:

Lord, have mercy.
Christ, have mercy.
Lord, have mercy.

Kyrie eleison.
Christe eleison.
Kyrie eleison.

Amy M. Edwards
Wichita, Kansas
February 2012

WEEK ONE: WE NEED GOD'S MERCY

ASH WEDNESDAY: JOHN THE BAPTIST PREACHES REPENTANCE

Read Matthew 3:1-12

Leader: Where did John the Baptist preach?

John the Baptist preached in the Wilderness of Judea.

Leader: What did he wear?

John the Baptist wore a camel-hair garment with a leather belt (verse 4).

Leader: What did he eat?

John the Baptist ate locusts and wild honey (verse 4).

Leader: Does anyone remember who John's parents were? (The answer is not in our reading today, but maybe you remember from other reading.)

Luke tells us that John was born to Zechariah and Elizabeth. Elizabeth was a relative of Mary, Jesus's mother.

Leader: What was John's message?

John's message was, "Repent, because the kingdom of heaven is at hand." (verse 2)

Leader: Why did he preach it urgently?

John warned the Pharisees and Sadducees about the coming wrath of God. Sin will be punished.

Leader: Look in verse 8. John said, "Bear fruit in keeping with repentance." What does this mean?

Bearing fruit in this verse isn't talking about oranges or apples. It's not even talking about evangelism, or making disciples, or having children. This is a reaping and sowing idea that takes place in your heart. If you plant a seed of repentance, what sort of plant will grow? It should have fruit that is evidence of repentance.

A repentant heart mourns over sin. Sometimes we are so sad about our sin that we feel real grief. We don't just regret what we did, we are deeply saddened about it. Because of this, we want to change and to turn away from our sinfulness. Grief or sadness about sin is fruit of repentance.

Leader: Why do you think that a repentant person usually reacts by praying something like, "Lord God, have mercy on me!"?

When we realize that we are hopelessly sinful, and we are deeply grieved for our sin, we also know that we can't change without help from God. With a real repentant heart, we beg God for mercy because we know that our sin deserves punishment, and we can't fix it by ourselves.

Leader: John told the Pharisees and Sadducees "Don't presume to say to yourselves, 'We have Abraham as our father.' For I tell you that God is able to raise up children for Abraham from these stones!" What do you think this means?

The Pharisees were not righteous before God simply because they descended from Abraham. You cannot be righteous before God because of who your mom or dad is.

Leader: What does this teach you?

Having Christian parents or going to a good church will not qualify you before God. When John says "raise up children for Abraham," he means spiritual children, or those who will be accepted into God's kingdom.

Leader: What does John say that God can do?

John says God can make stones into children of Abraham. This tells us that it is God who makes us into His people, not anything that we do on our own.

Prayer

I'm going to give you a time to pray silently to God, then I'll close in prayer. Use this time to repent of sin and call on God for His mercy.

Lord God, have mercy on us, for we are sinners. Open our eyes to Your truth during the weeks leading up to Easter. May this family devotional time be a special time for our family and we ask You to work mightily in each of our hearts, that we might receive Your mercy.

THURSDAY: JESUS, THE LAMB OF GOD

Read John 1:29-36

Leader: When John saw Jesus, what did he call Him?

John called Jesus the Lamb of God (verse 29, 36). John also called Jesus the Son of God (verse 34).

Leader: What did John say that the Lamb of God does?

The Lamb of God takes away the sin of the world (verse 29).

Leader: In verse 30 John says that Jesus is the One who ranks above John and that He existed before John. What did John say was proof that Jesus was greater than John?

In verse 32 John tells about seeing the amazing baptism of Jesus in which the Spirit descended from heaven like a dove and rested on Him. John tells this to prove that Jesus was in a different category from John.

Leader: Yesterday we talked about how true repentance makes us say, "Lord, have mercy." Why would you be very glad to see Jesus, who takes away sin, if you have a truly repentant heart?

We would be glad to see Jesus because when we realize the awfulness of our sin and our hopelessness, we know that we need God to save us. He has done just that, and sent Jesus, His Son to take away our sin! This is good news.

Leader: The term "Lamb of God" was full of meaning to the people John was talking to. Do you know what this meant to them?

All the Jewish people knew that they were required to sacrifice lambs, goats, and bulls to pay for their sins according to the law of God. Paying for sin by shedding the blood of an animal is called "atonement." Isaiah prophesied that the Suffering Servant, Jesus, would be "Like a lamb led to the slaughter" (Is. 53:7).

Prayer

Thank You, God, for Your great mercy in providing Jesus for us!

FRIDAY: THE TEMPTATION OF JESUS

Read Matthew 4:1-11

Leader: Who led Jesus into the desert to be tempted?

The Holy Spirit led Jesus into the wilderness or desert.

Leader: How long had Jesus fasted?

Jesus fasted for 40 days and 40 nights.

Leader: How did Jesus feel when the devil came to tempt Him?

Jesus was hungry when the devil came to tempt Him.

Leader: Why do you think that God led His Son to be tempted when He was so weak with hunger?

God did this to show that in the most difficult of all circumstances, Jesus did not sin.

Leader: How does this contrast to Adam and Eve's situation when they sinned?

Adam and Eve had all their needs met. They lived in the perfect abundance of the Garden of Eden when the devil came and tempted them. Adam and Eve fell into sin when it should have been easy to obey. Jesus did not sin when it could have been easy to sin.

Leader: How does this compare to your situation when you sin?

Although we don't enjoy the perfect circumstances of Adam and Eve, we are not under the same pressure and trial that Christ experienced in the desert.

Leader: Why do you think it was important for Jesus to show that He was sinless? Have you read any other Scriptures that talk about this?

God sent His Son Jesus to sacrifice Him for our sins. He could not bear our punishment as a substitute if He were a sinner, just as we are. Older kids or teens might remember Hebrews 7:26-28:

> For it was indeed fitting that we should have such a high priest, holy, innocent, unstained, separated from sinners, and exalted above the heavens. He has no need, like those high priests, to offer sacrifices daily, first for his own sins and then for those of the people, since he did this once for all when he offered up himself. For the law appoints men in their weakness as high priests, but the word of the oath, which came later than the law, appoints a Son who has been made perfect forever. He was just what we needed to intercede for us: holy, innocent, and undefiled.

Leader: What were the three things that the tempter challenged Jesus to do?

Change stones to bread (verse 3);

Throw yourself down from the Temple (verse 5-6);

Worship the devil in exchange for the world (verse 7-8)

Leader: How did Jesus respond to each temptation?

Jesus responded to each temptation by quoting Scripture.

Leader: Unlike Jesus, we are sinful people. There is no victory over sin apart from the power of Christ. We need His mercy and salvation. If we have put our faith in Christ, we can follow Christ's example and fight temptation with Scripture. Psalm 119:11 tells us, "I have stored up your word in my heart, that I might not sin against you."

Prayer

Thank You, Lord God, for sending Your Son Jesus to be our salvation. Thank You for suffering in the desert for our sake. We ask You to please work a miracle in the heart of [say each family member's name], enabling them to call on the mercy of Christ. With Your grace, we ask that You would help us to fight temptation with Your Scriptures.

Saturday: The Beatitudes

Read Matthew 5:1-12

Leader: What does it mean to be poor?

A poor person does not have money. A poor person is someone in need or in want.

Leader: Why are the poor in spirit blessed?

The poor in spirit are blessed because the kingdom of heaven is theirs.

Leader: What is the kingdom of heaven?

This is the non-earthly kingdom of people who belong to God. If you "have" or "belong to" the kingdom of heaven, you have put your faith in Jesus Christ. It means that you have eternal life and are no longer dead in your sins.

Leader: What does it mean to be poor in spirit?

Being poor in spirit means that we have a sense of hopelessness in our sin and we are ready to beg for God's mercy and forgiveness.

Leader: Why did Jesus say that the kingdom of heaven belongs to people who are poor in spirit?

This takes us back to our first discussion about repentance. In order to "have" the kingdom of heaven, we must believe in Jesus Christ, but in order to believe in Him, we must know that we are hopeless in our sin without Him.

Leader: What will God do for those who mourn?

God will comfort those who mourn.

Leader: Some translations call meek, "gentle." What will the meek, or gentle, inherit?

The meek will inherit the earth.

Leader: What kind of hunger and thirst does Jesus say will be satisfied?

Hunger and thirst for righteousness will be satisfied.

Leader: Think about people we know who don't believe in Jesus. Do you notice that they are searching for happiness? We also say they are searching for satisfaction. How can you tell?

(Answers will vary.) We see people try to be happy or satisfied by making lots of money, buying nice things, collecting toys or wealth. People often try to satisfy themselves through relationships with others, but because we are all sinners these relationships inevitably disappoint. People might suffer broken relationships, estrangements, bitterness, or divorce because they find that they can not be satisfied, or filled.

Leader: How will you be different from others without Christ when you hunger and thirst for righteousness?

If you hunger and thirst for righteousness, you will be satisfied in Jesus. You will be content. You will be able to be satisfied without collecting more and more things. You will be able to forgive and trust Jesus when other people disappoint you, knowing that you are just like them, a sinner in need of God's mercy.

Prayer

Almighty God, I ask that You would change us to be poor in spirit, that the kingdom of heaven would be ours. I pray that each one of us would hunger and thirst for righteousness and be satisfied forever in Jesus.

WEEK TWO: JESUS IS HOLY; WE ARE NOT

MONDAY: JUDGMENT FOR NAME CALLING

Read Matthew 5:21-26

Leader: This passage is part of Jesus' Sermon on the Mount. We read today that Jesus said that their ancestors were taught, "Do not murder." When and how did God command the Israelites not to murder?

When God gave Moses and the people the Ten Commandments, one of the commandments was, "You shall not murder."

Leader: According to Jesus, what was the consequence of murder under the Law?

The Law says, "Whoever murders will be liable to judgment."

Leader: What does "liable" mean?

"Liable" means to be legally held responsible. This means that the law holds you accountable for what you did.

Leader: We haven't committed murder, but Jesus has something to say about the way we treat our brothers. What does he say about calling a brother "fool"?

Jesus says that whoever does this will be subject to the court, or council, and hellfire.

Leader: Wow. That's pretty serious. Who does Jesus mean when he says "brother"?

When Jesus says "brother" He means brother or sister or friend or neighbor, another human being.

Leader: Everyone has been angry and called someone a name, either out loud or silently in their heart. According to Jesus, what is the consequence of this sin?

When we call someone a bad name, Jesus says we deserve judgment.

Leader: What is the only kind of person, then, would not be subject to judgment or hell?

A perfect person would not be subject to hell.

Leader: Since no one is perfect, what do you think Jesus wants to teach his listeners?

Jesus is teaching his listeners that God requires complete holiness of His people. However, it is obvious that no one can be perfectly holy. Only when we see that truth can we be poor in spirit, as we discussed on Saturday.

Leader: If it is impossible to be perfect, what should we do about these commands?

Repentant people who have received God's mercy will hunger and thirst for righteousness. We will want to do what is right, even if we continue to fail. Jesus changes the hearts of those who call on His Name, making them more and more perfect, like Him, as they seek Him. We won't ever be truly perfect while we're in our earthly bodies, but God is looking for hearts that are repentant and people who want to be perfect.

Prayer

Father God, forgive us for the name-calling that we have done. We are sinners and deserve Your judgment. We ask for Your forgiveness and ask that You would help us treat others with honor and love.

Tuesday: Love your Enemies

Read Matthew 5:43-48

Leader: Who does Jesus say that we should love?

We should love our enemies.

Leader: Who should we pray for?

We should pray for those who persecute us.

Leader: What does it mean that God causes the sun to rise on the evil and the good?

The sun is a blessing from God that gives warmth, energy, and light. Without the sun, we would die. God gives this blessing to all people, both those who do not believe in Him (the evil), and those who do believe in Him (the good).

What does it mean that He causes rain to fall on the evil and the good?

The rain is a blessing from God that gives water to all living things--plants, animals, and people. Without water, we would die. God gives this blessing to all people, both those who do not believe in Him (the evil), and those who do believe in Him (the good).

Leader: We have not done anything to earn or deserve the gifts of the sun and rain. These freely given gifts from God are called "common grace." It is God's grace that is given to all people.

Leader: Do you have any enemies?

(Answers will vary. Even those kids who don't seem to have an enemy probably have people in their lives who are sometimes mean or hurtful and might briefly be seen as an enemy.) Because we are all sinful people, even our friends sometimes are against us and hurt us, like an enemy would do.

Leader: Do you think that Jesus is talking about nations who are enemies of other nations?

These commands are speaking of individuals, not nations.

Leader: How is it possible for you to love an enemy?

It isn't possible to love our enemies unless we have Jesus as our Savior, giving us the strength and power to do what is unnatural to us. However, when we have realized our own sinfulness, our attitude toward the hurtful sin of others against us changes. We are able to be merciful rather than offended, forgiving rather than judgmental.

Leader: Who are some people that have hurt you or persecuted you that we can pray for right now?

(Listen as your kids share times of hurt, opposition, or persecution. Be compassionate to their hurts but model forgiveness toward the offender.)

Prayer

We are going to go around and pray by name for someone who has hurt you, then I'll close in prayer.

Almighty God, we don't know how to love enemies and pray for those who hurt us unless You give us the power to do it. Please change us and fill us with love and mercy for our enemies.

WEDNESDAY: THE LORD'S PRAYER

Read Matthew 6:9-15

Leader: Jesus gave us this prayer as a model of how we should pray. What is the first phrase of the prayer?

"Our Father in heaven."

Leader: Why might it be important for us to address God as "in heaven"?

By addressing God as "in heaven" we show that we understand His power and authority over us. We are not equals with God.

Leader: What does "hallowed be your name" mean?

Hallowed means to honor as holy. It is a verb, an action. Jesus wants us to honor God's name as holy, but He also wants us to pray that God's name would be honored as holy by everyone.

Leader: What does it mean to pray that God's kingdom would come, His will be done?

To pray, "Your kingdom come, Your will be done," means that we desire what God desires for ourselves, our family, and our community. We should pray this way because Jesus wants us to want the righteous rule of God.

Leader: When you hear about horrible things in the news, why is it a godly response to pray that God's kingdom would come, His will be done?

When we understand that God is holy and that we are not holy at all, bad news will not be a surprise to us in any way. However, it should prompt us to pray that God's kingdom would come. We should want Him to rule over us, knowing that He is right in all His ways.

Leader: What do we ask for daily?

God tells us to ask daily for our bread.

Leader: Why does Jesus tell us to ask for this each day?

We need to understand that all that we have, each day, comes from God. Our physical food and our spiritual food are all from God.

Leader: When in the Bible did God give bread to His people each day?

God provided manna to the Israelites in the wilderness.

Leader: What does this have to do with us?

*In the wilderness God only provided enough for each day. This applies to us spiritually because we need God to give us **each** day the spiritual food that we need to make it through the day, resisting sin and bringing glory to God.*

Leader: Jesus is called the Word and the Bread of Life in the book of John. Knowing this, what does the prayer about daily bread teach you about your Bible reading habits?

We need God's Word and Jesus daily.

Leader: What are debts?

Debts are sins against God, sins against others, sins against us.

Leader: Who are debtors?

Debtors are people who owe us something. This means that they have sinned against us.

Leader: Why does Jesus link together our request for forgiveness with the forgiveness that we have given others?

If we don't have forgiveness in our hearts for others, then we are not sincerely repentant. When we know that we are sinners who need the Lord's mercy (remember last week's devotions), we know that others are just as sinful and just as helpless to be righteous as we are. This gives us the ability to forgive.

Prayer

Let's say the Lord's Prayer aloud together and then I'll pray.

> Our Father in heaven,
> hallowed be your name.
> Your kingdom come,
> your will be done,
> on earth as it is in heaven.
> Give us this day our daily bread,
> and forgive us our debts,
> as we also have forgiven our debtors.
> And lead us not into temptation,
> but deliver us from evil.

Father God, teach each of us to honor Your Name above all things. Keep us faithful to turn to You for spiritual food in the Bible each day.

Thursday: Fasting

Read Matthew 6:16-18

Leader: What is fasting?

Fasting is going without something, usually food.

Leader: Why might a Christian fast?

Fasting is something that we are told to do sometimes when we pray. It is a way of focusing our worship onto Christ alone. Fasting is an outward sign that we acknowledge our need for God's mercy.

Leader: What is a hypocrite?

A hypocrite is someone who tells everyone to behave a certain way, but doesn't follow that way himself.

Leader: What does Jesus say that these hypocrites are doing?

These hypocrites are making a big deal out of their fasting, showing everyone that they are "suffering" by fasting.

Leader: What does Jesus say you should do when you fast?

When you fast you should wash your face as usual. Do not look out of the ordinary. Your fasting should be known only to you and God.

Leader: What is the purpose of fasting?

Fasting is linked in the Bible with prayers of repentance (showing grief over sin), and with prayers of supplication (asking fervently for something). It is usually a private action, although in some places (such as Ezra 8) the people are told to fast together. Fasting is a way of focusing fully on Jesus.

Leader: Fasting is unusual today, but some people traditionally fast during Lent. Many people give up a particular favorite food or activity during the 40 days before Easter. If you are fasting from something during this time of Lent, how can you do so while obeying Jesus's instructions?

(Discuss with your family what it might be like to fast without others knowing.)

Leader: The important thing in this passage is that we are truly worshipping God from our hearts and not just to impress other people. Let's ask God to show us if our hearts are genuinely worshipping or if we are doing it to impress those around us.

Prayer

Lord, I pray that you would make us genuinely repentant. Let our worship be sincere. Show us if we are more concerned about impressing others than seeking You.

FRIDAY: TREASURES IN HEAVEN

Read Matthew 6:19-20

Leader: What does it mean to "lay up for yourself treasures"?

To "lay up for yourself treasure," means to collect, gather, save, or hoard treasure.

Leader: We'll go around and I want each of you to name an earthly treasure.

This could be money, gold, clothing, books, video games, toys, cars, jewelry, stuffed animals. Treasure is anything that we greatly value. "On earth" means that it is temporary.

Leader: Treasures on earth are also known as "temporal things." Temporal means that it is temporary. It will not last. To show you that temporal things do not last, what does Jesus tell you will happen to treasures on earth?

Moth and rust destroy treasures and thieves take them, too.

Leader: What kind of treasure does Jesus say that you should store up?

Jesus says we should store up treasures in heaven.

Leader: What do you think that heavenly treasures are?

Heavenly treasures are eternal life in Christ and victory over sin, which leads to death.

Leader: Heavenly treasures are often known as "eternal things" (in contrast to temporal things). They cannot be destroyed by moths or rust or be taken by thieves. When Jesus says to collect treasures in heaven, what do you think He means?

Jesus means we should search after eternal life. Jesus Christ Himself is the only thing that lasts or that satisfies.

Leader: How can we collect eternal treasure?

There is only one way to collect eternal treasure. It is to trust in Christ as your Savior and live your life for Him.

Leader: Are we collecting eternal treasure when we do good things, like obey, give to others, serve at church, etc.?

*Maybe and maybe not. Help your family see that only those things that we do by the power of Christ after we've trusted Him as our Savior will be "eternal treasure." If we do these things to show off or because we think they will help convince Jesus to take us to heaven, they are **not** eternal treasure.*

Leader: What do these verses from I Corinthians 3:11-15 have to do with this?

1 Corinthians 3:11-15

> For no one can lay a foundation other than that which is laid, which is Jesus Christ. Now if anyone builds on the foundation with gold, silver, precious stones, wood, hay, straw— each one's work will become manifest, for the Day will disclose it, because it will be revealed by fire, and the fire will test what sort of work each one has done. If the work that anyone has built on the foundation survives, he will receive a reward. If anyone's work is burned up, he will suffer loss, though he himself will be saved, but only as through fire."

It is important to see that Jesus Himself is our treasure. Doing "good deeds" is only an eternal treasure if it is done by the power of Christ. We can't add to our eternal treasure in our own strength. Good deeds done by those who are not in the kingdom of God are temporal treasures, not eternal treasures.

Leader: When we focus on temporal things (treasures on earth) more than Christ, God calls this something sinful. Do you know what word the Bible uses for this?

Focusing on temporal things is called idolatry.

Leader: You could say that there are only two ways to live, collecting eternal treasure or collecting temporal treasure. What do you think it looks like to live your life collecting eternal treasure and not temporal treasure?

(Help your family to think specifically about their own lives in the midst of school, work, the neighborhood, sports, etc. Gently prompt them to consider areas of their lives that might fall in the category of temporal treasure. Discuss specific ways that your kids might put Christ above temporal things.)

Prayer

Father God, forgive us for collecting earthly treasure and valuing it above You. We want **You** as our treasure. May Your grace be showered on us so that the appeal of earthly treasure will fade away in our sight next to the glory of You.

SATURDAY: THE WIDE AND NARROW GATES

Read Matthew 7:13-23

Leader: Where does the wide gate and easy road lead?

The wide gate and easy road leads to destruction.

Leader: Where does the narrow gate and hard road lead?

The narrow gate and hard road leads to life.

Leader: This seems to mean that we must work hard to be saved, but if that were true, it would contradict, or disagree with, other Scripture. Think back to our discussions about John the Baptist and repentance. Why do you think that Jesus says that the road to life is hard and few find it?

The hardest thing for anyone to do is repent and admit that they are helpless before a holy God. In fact, no one does this without the Holy Spirit's miraculous work in their heart, changing them and opening their eyes to their sin and God's holiness. Because of this, Jesus teaches us that we shouldn't be surprised that few find the way to life.

Leader: What is a false prophet?

A false prophet is anyone who teaches something other than the gospel of Jesus Christ.

Leader: Why does Jesus say that false prophets come in sheep's clothing but inside are wolves?

When Jesus says false prophets come in sheep's clothing but are actually wolves, He means that they are very dangerous to us, as a wolf is dangerous to a sheep. We are easily tricked into thinking that false prophets are trustworthy and teaching us good things.

Leader: How can we recognize a false prophet (look at verse 20)?

We can recognize false prophets by their fruit.

Leader: What does this mean?

Genuine believers in Christ will live a godly life that brings glory and honor to God, not to themselves. They will live and teach in accordance to Scripture.

Leader: Jesus says that some people will think they know Him, but will be told, "I never knew you, depart from me," (verse 23). Think back to the wide and narrow gates. What do you think this means?

Many people think that they are pleasing God by doing what is right or doing good things. Some even think that because they agree that Jesus died for their sins, they are on the narrow road, but knowing something in your head isn't the same as trusting in Christ for salvation. Doing something good in your own strength is not even "good" in the eyes of God.

Leader: Yesterday we read I Corinthians 3:11-15. How does this connect with our reading today?

Only fruit that is built on a foundation of Jesus Christ will be revealed as "good fruit." Even kindness and charitable acts done by those who reject Jesus will be revealed as "bad fruit."

Prayer

Lord God, may Your Holy Spirit open our eyes to Your truth. Help us examine our hearts and see if we are trusting in Christ or if we are trusting in our own works.

WEEK THREE: JESUS IS GOD AND HAS THE POWER TO HEAL AND SAVE

MONDAY: WATER INTO WINE

Read John 2:1-11

Leader: What event was happening in this passage?

In this passage, Jesus, His mother, and His disciples went to a wedding.

Leader: Where was the wedding?

The wedding was in Cana, a town in Galilee.

Leader: What happened at the wedding?

The wine ran out at the wedding.

Leader: Who told Jesus that the wine ran out?

Jesus' mother told Him that the wine ran out.

Leader: How did Jesus respond to this news?

He told His mother that "My hour has not yet come," but Mary, Jesus' mother, told the servants to follow His instructions anyway.

Leader: What were the stone water jars for?

The stone water jars were for the Jewish rites of purification. These were cleansing, or washing, rituals that required water.

Leader: Jesus gave what instruction?

Jesus instructed, "Fill the jars with water, draw some out and give it to the master of the wedding feast."

Leader: To whom did Jesus give this instruction?

Jesus gave this instruction to the servants.

Leader: What did the master of the feast say about the wine?

The master of the feast told the bridegroom that it was the best wine of the feast, much better than the wine that had run out.

Leader: What is water?

Water is collected from rain, rivers, lakes, or wells.

Leader: What is wine?

Wine is made from the juice of grapes.

Leader: Is water used to make wine like it is used to make tea or coffee?

Although grapevines need water to produce grapes, which are pressed and made into wine, wine is not something mixed with water like tea or coffee.

Leader: Is it possible to explain this change of water into wine with the natural laws of the universe, that is, by science?

No, this miracle that happened to the water doesn't make any sense scientifically, or naturally. It is supernatural, which means above or outside of nature.

Leader: Verse 11 calls this the first of Jesus's signs. What was this a sign of?

Jesus showed everyone that He had supernatural power to transform water into something entirely different through the power of His Word. Only Someone who was not confined by the natural laws of science could do something like that. This miracle is a sign that Jesus has divine power. He is God.

Leader: What does John call it in verse 11?

John calls it a manifestation of His glory.

Leader: What was the response of the disciples who saw this happen?

After this miracle the disciples believed in Jesus. They knew that Jesus was the Messiah, the anointed one of God.

Leader: What should be your response when you witness evidence that Jesus is God?

If we witness evidence that Jesus is God, we would believe that Jesus is God.

Prayer

Almighty God, thank You for sending your Son Jesus. Thank You that Jesus was not just a special man, but He is God. Open our eyes to this truth, that we might be able to believe in Jesus Christ.

Tuesday: A Leper Healed

Read Matthew 8:1-4

Leader: What was the man's problem?

The man had leprosy, a skin disease.

Leader: From what you know about the Old Testament, what was the Jewish attitude toward lepers? (See Leviticus 13 and 14.)

Lepers were considered "unclean" and were sent out of the community. The Law gave specific and detailed instructions about how those with skin diseases could be cleansed or healed from their impurity and restored to the community.

Leader: Why do you think God made rules that declared people unclean because of a skin disease?

This rule, that people with a skin disease are unclean, taught the people that God is pure and holy. A skin disease represents a contamination.

Leader: What did the leper say to Jesus?

The leper said, "Lord, if you will, you can make me clean."

Leader: What does this tell you about the leper's belief about Jesus?

The leper believed that Jesus had the power to make him clean and heal his disease.

Leader: You and I likely do not have leprosy or a serious skin disease, but what sort of cleansing do we need?

We each need cleansing from our sin, which has contaminated us.

Leader: How did Jesus respond to the leper's humble request?

Jesus immediately cleansed the leper (verse 3), which means that He healed him.

Leader: What can Jesus do for you?

(Tenderly guide your family in a discussion about their sins and their need for Jesus to cleanse their hearts. Sometimes children assume that they are saved from their sin because they are good. Gently lead them to examine their hearts and consider if they are trying to cleanse their own sin and "be good" apart from Christ.)

Leader: Do you believe that Jesus can do it?

(Answers may vary. Don't criticize answers or assume that everyone does believe it.)

Leader: Even if you *say* that Jesus can do it, are you living like you believe that or are you trying to cleanse yourself?

(Answers will vary. Talk this through with your kids, as time allows.)

Prayer

I'm going to give you a moment of silence in which to ask God to cleanse, or heal, your heart. If you have realized today that you haven't been trusting Christ, but have been trusting in your own goodness, take a minute to privately tell Jesus and ask His forgiveness.

Lord God, I pray that You would miraculously work in the hearts of [say each family member's name]. May we be healed from sin and trusting in Your power to cleanse and heal.

WEDNESDAY: THE CENTURION'S SICK SERVANT

Read Luke 7:1-10

Leader: Who had a sick servant?

A centurion had a sick servant.

Leader: What is a centurion?

A centurion is a man who commanded 100 men in the Roman army.

Leader: Would this be a Jewish man or a Gentile man?

A centurion would be a Gentile, not a Jew.

Leader: Why do you think that the centurion sent Jewish leaders to ask Jesus to heal his servant?

The centurion probably figured that Jesus would be more likely to help him if Jewish leaders represented him. This is why he sent Jewish leaders to ask Jesus for him.

Leader: What did the Jewish leaders tell Jesus?

The Jewish leaders told Jesus, "He is worthy to have you do this for him, for he loves our nation, and he is the one who built us our synagogue."

Leader: What do you think about this statement? What does it tell you about the Jewish leaders who served as the messengers of the centurion?

*The Jewish leaders seemed to think that to receive a miraculous gift of healing, it was necessary to prove that one was **worthy** of the gift, especially since the centurion was not already one of the Jewish people, who were special to God. They wanted to convince Jesus that the centurion, who was not a Jew, should still be given a gift of healing.*

This statement shows us that the Jewish leaders assumed that they could earn God's favor either through works or by their Jewish heritage.

Leader: How can you tell that the centurion didn't share this view?

The centurion understood he was unworthy of God's favor, but He also knew that Jesus held power and authority to heal. He had faith that Jesus could heal his servant because of who Jesus was, not because of who the centurion was.

Leader: How did Jesus describe the centurion's attitude compared to that of the Jewish leaders?

Jesus called the centurion's faith greater than any in Israel.

Leader: What do you learn about Jesus from this event?

Jesus again showed His supernatural, divine power. He is God and has authority over the physical world, including illness and disease.

Leader: What do you learn about our relationship with Jesus through this event?

Jesus responds to faith, not to works. Salvation comes to us through our faith, even though we are unworthy of Him. We cannot impress Him with our deeds and actions, even if we seem like an honorable person to our family and friends.

Prayer

Almighty God, You hold the power over all creation, even over the tiniest germs. Thank You for this text which shows us that Jesus Christ has authority over all things. I pray that You would increase our faith and that [say each family member's name] would be confident in Jesus.

Thursday: The Wind and Waves

Read Matthew 8:23-27

Leader: Jesus and His disciples got into boat. Then what happened?

A great storm arose, swamping the boat with waves.

Leader: What was Jesus doing at the time?

Jesus was sleeping during the storm.

Leader: What does this teach you about Jesus?

Jesus was human and needed rest and sleep.

Leader: What did the disciples do when the storm swamped their boat?

When their boat was swamped, they awakened Jesus and pleaded with Him to save them. They were sure that their boat was doomed and probably were frustrated that Jesus was sleeping through the crisis.

Leader: Even though the disciples asked Jesus to save them, He said they had little faith. Why?

The disciples' panicky fear revealed that they didn't trust that Jesus could actually save them from their situation.

Leader: In spite of the disciples' lack of faith, Jesus rebuked the winds and the sea and a great calm came over the water. What does this teach you about Jesus?

Jesus has power over the natural world, including weather patterns. The weather obeyed His Word. This proves that Jesus is God and while He was fully human, He was also fully God.

Leader: John 3:36 says,

> Whoever believes in the Son has eternal life,
> but whoever rejects the Son will not see life,
> for God's wrath remains on him." (NIV 1984)

In light of this verse, why does it matter that Jesus holds power over the weather?

The Bible teaches us that we must believe in Jesus Christ as the Son of God in order to escape God's wrath (or punishment) for sin. When Jesus commanded the wind and the waves, He proved that He is God and has the power and authority to command weather and give eternal life.

Leader: What was the response of the disciples to Jesus's action?

The disciples marveled and said, "What sort of man is this, that even winds and sea obey him?" This showed that they realized that they had just witnessed an act of God, not man.

Leader: Try to explain how this event can teach you something about what you need Jesus to do in your life. What does this have to do with the Gospel and salvation?

(Help your family see that before putting faith in Christ we are like the disciples, in a doomed boat. We are powerless to battle the consequence of sin and it has trapped us in a sinking ship, just as the weather had trapped the disciples in a sinking ship. Only Jesus has the power to reverse our situation and save us from our sin. Like the disciples, we can be confident in His power and His divinity because of this event.)

Prayer

Thank You, God, for Your Son Jesus. Thank You for showing us through this event that Jesus is the Christ, the Son of God, who holds power over all creation, even the wind and the waves. This shows us the power of Jesus, that He is God and has the power and authority to save us from our sin. May our faith in You be stronger today.

FRIDAY: JESUS WALKS ON WATER

Read Matthew 14:22-33

Leader: Jesus commanded the disciples to get in their boat and cross the lake. What did Jesus do, rather than go with them?

Jesus went up on the mountain by Himself to pray.

Leader: What happened to the disciples in the meantime?

The disciples' boat was a long way from the shore, beaten by the waves, with the wind against them.

Leader: What did the disciples need?

Once again, the disciples were in need of help.

Leader: What did Jesus do?

Jesus came to them across the water, walking on the water.

Leader: How did the disciples react to this?

The disciples were afraid and in shock.

Leader: How did Jesus show mercy to them at that moment?

Verse 27 says, "He spoke to them, saying 'Take heart; it is I. Do not be afraid.'" Jesus mercifully comforted the disciples with His voice.

Leader: What does this teach you about Jesus?

Jesus has power to save and *Jesus has the power to comfort. He tenderly cares about us and our feelings.*

Leader: What did Peter say and then do?

Peter asked Jesus, "Lord, if it is you, command me to come to you on the water." Jesus did and then Peter stepped out of the boat.

Leader: Peter's confidence in Jesus faded away when the strong wind blew. What things are like a strong wind in your life, causing you to become afraid and lose your confidence in Jesus Christ?

(Help your family consider things going on in their lives this week, pressures they are feeling, fears they are having, or temptations to sin that seem impossible to resist.)

Leader: Jesus immediately reached for Peter and asked, "O you of little faith, why did you doubt?" Jesus is immediately reaching out to **you** to take **your** hand as you are sinking in those pressures, fears, and temptations of life. He is available to rescue you. Are you ready to receive His comfort and mercy? How did the disciples respond to Jesus Christ's tender love and mercy?

The disciples worshipped Him and called Him the Son of God.

Leader: We should respond to Jesus in worship and by declaring our belief that He is the Son of God. Is that your response to Him?

Prayer

Father God, I pray that we would take the hand of Jesus, that [say each family member's name] would take the hand of Jesus, put their faith and confidence in Him, and experience His comfort and mercy.

SATURDAY: A BLIND MAN SEES

Read Luke 18: 35-43

Leader: What was the blind man doing by the side of the road?

The blind man was begging.

Leader: When the blind man heard the crowd and asked about it, what was he told?

The blind man was told that Jesus of Nazareth was passing by (verse 37).

Leader: What did the blind man say when he heard this news?

The blind man cried out "Jesus, Son of David, have mercy on me!" (Verse 38)

Leader: What does it mean that the blind man called Jesus "Son of David"?

This title is another way of calling Jesus the Messiah of the Old Testament. Somehow the blind man is acknowledging that Jesus is the Son of God and He is the fulfillment of Old Testament prophecies about the Anointed One (Messiah) who would come from the line of David.

Leader: The blind man begged Jesus for mercy and he said, "Let me recover my sight." What problem did the blind man have?

The blind man could not see.

Leader: What problem do you have without Christ?

In the same way, without the power of Jesus, we cannot see the truth of Who He is and our need for Him. We need to be given spiritual sight.

Leader: What did Jesus do for him and why?

Jesus gave him his sight and told him that his faith made him well.

Leader: Maybe you are spiritually blind right now. If so, what can you do?

A spiritually blind person can beg Jesus for mercy and for sight and put their faith in Him.

Leader: How should you pray for your friends or family that are spiritually blind and do not believe that Jesus is the Son of God?

We should pray that Jesus would give them sight that they might see Him and believe. We should pray that God would put faith in their hearts.

Leader: What happened immediately to the blind man and how did he respond?

He could see, and then he followed Jesus and glorified God.

Leader: How can you follow Jesus and glorify God right now?

(Help your family think specifically about their lives and how they can glorify God for what He has done in their lives.)

Prayer

I'm going to give each of you an opportunity to pray aloud, praising God for His mercy in giving you spiritual sight. All you have to do is say something like, "I praise You, God, for giving me eyes to see and to believe in Jesus."

O Lord, You are the great Healer, in our mercy, healing our spiritual blindness and giving us spiritual sight. We humbly ask You to work this same miracle in the lives of [say the names of friends and family who do not believe in Christ].

WEEK FOUR: JESUS IS THE MESSIAH, THE SON OF MAN

MONDAY: JESUS, THE SON OF MAN

Read John 1:43-51

Leader: In this passage, what was the name of the man that Jesus asked to follow Him?

Philip was the man Jesus called to follow Him.

Leader: Philip was from the town of Bethsaida. Who was also from that town?

Andrew and Peter were also from Bethsaida.

Leader: Who are Andrew and Peter?

Andrew and Peter are brothers that Jesus called as His disciples. This is recorded in the verses just before the passage we read today.

Leader: Who did Philip find and tell about Jesus?

Philip found Nathanael and told him about Jesus.

Leader: What did Philip tell Nathanael about Jesus?

Philip said, "We have found him of whom Moses in the Law and also the prophets wrote, Jesus of Nazareth, the son of Joseph." (Verse 45)

Leader: What did Nathanael have to say about this?

Nathanael asked, "Can anything good come out of Nazareth?" He was skeptical about Jesus because people looked down on the town of Nazareth as a lowly town.

Leader: What happened to change Nathanael's mind about Jesus?

Jesus complimented Nathanael and then showed that He supernaturally already knew what Nathanael was doing when Nathanael knew Jesus wasn't looking. This showed Nathanael that Jesus was the Son of God because He had divine knowledge of things that were not before His eyes.

Leader: This week we are going to find out what it means that Jesus was called the "Son of Man." After Nathanael was amazed that Jesus knew he was under the fig tree, Jesus told him that he would see much greater things than that. What did Jesus say that Nathanael would see?

Jesus said Nathanael would see heaven opened and the angels of God ascending and descending, going up and down, on the Son of Man.

Leader: What does heaven being opened and angels going up and down remind you of?

This answer reminds us of the passage in Genesis 28:10-13 where Jacob had a special dream about a stairway reaching to heaven.

Leader: Let me read the passage from Genesis about this dream.

> Jacob left Beersheba and went toward Haran.
> And he came to a certain place and stayed
> there that night, because the sun had set.
> Taking one of the stones of the place, he put it
> under his head and lay down in that place to
> sleep. And he dreamed, and behold, there was
> a ladder set up on the earth, and the top of it
> reached to heaven. And behold, the angels of
> God were ascending and descending on it!
> And behold, the LORD stood above it and
> said, "I am the LORD, the God of Abraham

your father and the God of Isaac. The land on
which you lie I will give to you and to your
offspring. Your offspring shall be like the dust
of the earth, and you shall spread abroad to
the west and to the east and to the north and
to the south, and in you and your offspring
shall all the families of the earth be blessed.

Leader: In our passage today Jesus said that angels of God were
ascending (going up) and descending (going down) **on** the Son of
Man. What do you think Jesus meant?

*Jesus meant that the Son of Man would be the stairway to God. The Son of
Man would become a way to be with God. Jesus didn't explain this fully to
Nathanael at this time, but by comparing the Son of Man to Jacob's stairway (or
ladder), He was making a very significant point. The Son of Man would be the
One in Jacob's offspring that would bless all families of the earth by being the
stairway to God.*

Leader: Why did Jesus use the title Son of Man to refer to
Himself?

*(Answers may vary. Listen to your family's ideas, then share this additional
information.) This title refers to Daniel 7:13-14 where Daniel saw a vision of
"one like a son of man" who came out of heaven. The Jewish people knew that
this very special man would be their Messiah, the Anointed One. When Jesus
spoke of the Son of Man, He meant the Messiah. In this way Jesus claimed that
He was the promised Messiah from God. The title "Son of Man" shows that
even though Jesus was God, He was at the same time a human being just like you
and me. This is hard to understand, but the Bible teaches us that this is true.*

Leader: These verses teach us that Jesus is the Son of Man, but
they also teach us something about how we can be with God. What
do you learn from these verses about how you can be with God?

It is only through Jesus, our stairway to heaven, that we can be with God.

Prayer

Father God, we praise and thank You for Jesus, who has made it
possible for us to know You. Thank You for sending Your Son for our

sake. Thank You for teaching us Your truth, that You provided a way for us to know You and that way is Jesus Christ.

TUESDAY: JESUS HEALS THE PARALYTIC

Read Luke 5:17-26

Leader: Who had come from every village of Galilee and Judea to listen to Jesus?

Pharisees and teachers of the law came to listen to Jesus.

Leader: What do you know about Pharisees and teachers of the law?

The Pharisees and teachers of the law were Jewish religious leaders. We know from this passage and others that they did not believe in Jesus. Although they knew the Scriptures, studied the Scriptures, and memorized the Scriptures, they did not know God.

Leader: Some men tried to bring a paralyzed man to Jesus, but what stopped them at first?

The men couldn't bring the paralyzed man to Jesus because it was too crowded, and they couldn't get through the crowd to Jesus.

Leader: What did the men do instead of giving up and going home?

The men went up to the roof and lowered the paralyzed man down through the tiles to see Jesus.

Leader: Seeing the paralyzed man, what did Jesus say to him?

Jesus said to the paralyzed man, "Man, your sins are forgiven you." (Verse 20)

Leader: Why did this event upset the Pharisees and scribes?

The Pharisees and scribes thought He was blaspheming. They said only God can forgive sins and they felt it dishonored God for a man to claim to forgive sins.

Leader: What is blasphemy?

Blasphemy is dishonoring God by misusing His name through cursing or swearing by His name.

Leader: Why was Jesus not blaspheming?

Jesus wasn't blaspheming because Jesus was God and had the authority to forgive sins.

Leader: How did Jesus know that the Pharisees were questioning His actions?

Jesus perceived their thoughts. (Verse 22) Jesus knows everyone's thoughts.

Leader: Who did Jesus say had the authority to forgive sins?

Jesus said the Son of Man, meaning Himself, had the authority to forgive sins.

Leader: How did Jesus prove to the Pharisees that He had the authority to forgive sins and that He was the Son of Man (a reference to the Messiah)?

Jesus proved Himself by telling the paralyzed man to get up and walk, which he immediately did.

Leader: Why does this prove that Jesus had authority to forgive sins?

Jesus showed evidence that He had supernatural power over the natural world and was not subject to the laws of the universe, like other humans, but instead the laws of the universe obeyed Jesus. He had the power to heal the man's physical body, which showed that He had the power to heal the man's spiritual soul, which was paralyzed by sin.

Leader: What did the paralyzed man do to be healed?

The paralyzed man did nothing to be healed. We can do nothing to heal ourselves except come to Jesus in our helplessness and, in faith, wait for Him to heal us.

Leader: Many people do not believe that Jesus was anything more than a great teacher. What do you think about the fact that the Pharisees, who knew the Old Testament probably better than you do, didn't *know* God and recognize His Son Jesus?

(Answers will vary. Point out that knowing the Bible isn't what saves us, even though it is true that we cannot know Jesus without the Bible. It is Jesus who does a miracle in our hearts, opening our eyes to truth, healing us from the sickness of sin, bringing our dead hearts alive again.)

Leader: The healed man went home glorifying God. What does this mean?

The healed man gave all the credit to God. He didn't take any credit for himself. He knew that he was healed only because of the power of Jesus Christ, not because of anything he had done.

Leader: What does this teach you about how you should give glory to God?

It is important that we always recognize that we are saved only because of God's mercy and grace, not because of our efforts. Likewise, after we have been saved by God and we begin to be sanctified (made holy), we should always give the glory to God knowing that any holiness that is evident in our lives is the work of God, not ourselves.

Prayer

Father God, We praise You because You gave Jesus Christ, your Son, the authority to forgive our sins. We are paralyzed by our sin until Jesus heals us. Lord, I pray that our friends and family who are still paralyzed by sin would be healed by You. We who have been healed from sin thank You and ask that you would make us more like You. We want to bring You glory in all we do and ask You to help us do that today.

WEDNESDAY: JESUS, THE LORD OF THE SABBATH

Read Luke 6:1-5

Leader: Today's reading tells about something that happened on a Sabbath. What is the Sabbath?

The Sabbath is the seventh day of the week. We call it Saturday.

Leader: What did Jesus' disciples do on a Sabbath that the Pharisees considered unlawful?

Jesus' disciples plucked grain, rubbed the heads in their hands to get rid of the chaff, and ate the grain.

Leader: What did the Pharisees ask Jesus?

The Pharisees asked, "Why are you doing what is not lawful to do on the Sabbath?"

Leader: What was God's commandment about the Sabbath?

God commanded the Israelites to "Remember the Sabbath day, to keep it holy. Six days you shall labor, and do all your work, but the seventh day is a Sabbath to the LORD your God. On it you shall not do any work..." (Exodus 20: 8-10a)

Leader: Why did the Pharisees think that Jesus's disciples broke this command by plucking and rubbing grain on the Sabbath?

Picking grain and rubbing off the chaff was considered work, a violation of the Sabbath. The Pharisees felt very smart and proud to be telling Jesus the rules of the Sabbath.

Leader: God is the author of the Law (the Ten Commandments) that He gave to Israel. Why do you think God commanded the Israelites to keep the Sabbath holy by resting from work?

The command to rest on the Sabbath day was a command of blessing to Israel.

Leader: What did Jesus tell the Pharisees?

Jesus asked them about the time that King David and his men entered the house of God and ate the bread of the Presence, which is not lawful for any but the priests to eat. Jesus also told the Pharisees that the Son of Man was Lord of the Sabbath.

Leader: What does it mean to be the lord, or master, of something?

The lord, or master, is in charge and sets the rules as well as enforces the rules.

Leader: When Jesus said that He was Lord of the Sabbath, what did Jesus mean?

*Jesus meant that, as Lord of the Sabbath, the command to keep the Sabbath holy was **His** command. Jesus is God. He gave the command to keep the Sabbath, and He alone decides what violates that command. It was not God who defined plucking grain and rubbing off the chaff as "work" and therefore unlawful. This was a human definition of God's command to not work on the Sabbath.*

Leader: Jesus said that He was Lord of the Sabbath. This statement meant that Jesus was equal to God and had authority over the Law. Why does it matter to us today that Jesus has authority over all things?

Jesus is not just a human being, He is God. He is not just a good man with wise teaching, He has authority over us. Many people deny His authority, but their denial doesn't alter the fact that He is Lord over all.

Leader: How should we respond to this truth?

(Answers will vary.) We should respond in worship, knowing that Jesus is Lord, and in submission to His authority over our lives.

Prayer

Jesus, You are Lord of all. Forgive us when we deny this truth! May we by Your grace, through faith, declare You Lord over every part of our lives.

THURSDAY: THE WHEAT AND THE WEEDS

Read Matthew 13:24-30, 36-43

Leader: Jesus told a parable, or story, comparing the kingdom of heaven to what?

Jesus compared the kingdom of heaven to a man who sowed good seed in a field, but while he was sleeping his enemy sowed weeds in among the wheat.

Leader: What happened when the plants sprouted?

When the plants sprouted and produced grain, weeds appeared among the grain.

Leader: What did the master's servants ask the master?

The servants asked, "Master, did you not sow good seed in your field? How then does it have weeds?" (Verse 27)

Leader: What did the master reply?

The master said, "An enemy has done this."

Leader: The servants were eager to gather up the weeds and pull them out of the field. What did the master say about this?

The master would not let them do this because he did not want any of the wheat uprooted in the process of pulling the weeds.

Leader: What did the master say should be done at harvest time?

The reapers should gather the weeds first, bind them in bundles to be burned, then gather the wheat into the barn.

Leader: Who asked Jesus to explain this parable, or story, to them?

The disciples asked Jesus to explain the parable about the wheat and the weeds. (Verse 36)

Leader: Who did Jesus say is the one sowing the good seed?

Jesus said that the Son of Man is the one who sows the good seed.

Leader: What did Jesus say that the field represents?

Jesus said the field is the world.

Leader: What did Jesus say the good seed represents?

The good seed represents the sons of the kingdom.

Leader: Who are the sons of the kingdom?

The sons of the kingdom are those who believe in Jesus and have been made righteous by Him.

Leader: Who are represented by the weeds?

The weeds represent the sons of the evil one, sown by the devil.

Leader: According to Jesus, what does the gathering of the harvest represent?

The gathering of the harvest represents the end of the age.

Leader: Who are represented by the reapers?

The reapers represent the angels of the Son of Man, who is Jesus.

Leader: What does Jesus say will happen at the end of the age?

The Son of Man will send His angels to gather out of His kingdom all causes of sin and law-breakers and throw them into the fiery furnace, where there is weeping and gnashing of teeth. The righteous, however, will shine like the sun in the kingdom of their Father. (Verses 41-43)

Leader: There are some false teachers today who argue that there is no evidence for hell and that all people will be saved. What do you think about that in light of this teaching from Jesus, the Son of God?

The idea that all are saved and that there is no hell cannot be reconciled with the teaching of this parable. Jesus made it clear that the weeds would be thrown into a fiery furnace where there is weeping and gnashing of teeth. Clearly there is an eternal destination for the people who are law-breakers or sons of the evil one. It is a miserable place apart from God.

Leader: According to this parable, there are only two kinds of people in the world: the wheat and the weeds. The wheat represents all believers in Jesus Christ and the weeds represent all those evildoers who are against Jesus Christ. When we look at our world today, with all of the injustice, wickedness, and suffering, why do you think that Jesus doesn't just come and destroy all the weeds right away, right now?

Jesus said that pulling the weeds too soon could damage the wheat. He is waiting to judge the world in order that all of His people might come to Him. 2 Peter 3:9 says this:

> The Lord is not slow to fulfill his promise as
> some count slowness, but is patient toward
> you, not wishing that any should perish, but
> that all should reach repentance.

Leader: How can you be certain that you are among the wheat, the children of the kingdom of God who will be safe with Jesus, and not among the weeds, the children of the evil one destined for judgment?

(Listen to your family's answers. Here are some verses from Romans to help focus on the truth of the good news, the Gospel.)

Romans 8:1 assures us, "There is therefore now no condemnation for those who are in Christ Jesus."

Romans 5:8-10 explains why being "in Christ Jesus" saves us from condemnation:

> but God shows his love for us in that while we were still sinners, Christ died for us. Since, therefore, we have now been justified by his blood, much more shall we be saved by him from the wrath of God. For if while we were enemies we were reconciled to God by the death of his Son, much more, now that we are reconciled, shall we be saved by his life.

Romans 10:9 explains how we know that we are among those justified:

> because, if you confess with your mouth that Jesus is Lord and believe in your heart that God raised him from the dead, you will be saved.

Prayer

Almighty, Sovereign God, we tremble at the truth that there will be a judgment day and that many will not be saved from Your wrath against sin and wickedness. May we each fall on our knees before You now, asking for Your mercy and forgiveness, and declaring our faith in Jesus our Lord.

FRIDAY: THE SNAKE ON A POLE

Read John 3:9-18

Leader: Who was Nicodemus?

Nicodemus was a Pharisee, a teacher of Israel and a ruler of the Jews. (For more detail, see John 3:1)

Leader: Jesus was speaking with Nicodemus in secret, at night, and told Nicodemus that no one has ascended into heaven except He who descended from heaven. Who did Jesus say descended, or came down from, heaven?

Only the Son of Man has come down from heaven.

Leader: Jesus said that Moses lifted something up in the wilderness. What was it?

Moses lifted up a serpent in the wilderness.

Leader: What did Jesus say must happen to the Son of Man?

The Son of Man must be lifted up, as was the serpent.

Leader: Do you know what Jesus was talking about when He mentioned the serpent that Moses lifted up?

(If your children remember this event from the Old Testament, give them time to explain.)

Leader: Numbers 21:5-9 says,

> And the people spoke against God and against
> Moses, "Why have you brought us up out of
> Egypt to die in the wilderness? For there is no
> food and no water, and we loathe this
> worthless food." Then the LORD sent fiery
> serpents among the people, and they bit the
> people, so that many people of Israel died.
> And the people came to Moses and said, "We
> have sinned, for we have spoken against the
> LORD and against you. Pray to the LORD,
> that he take away the serpents from us." So
> Moses prayed for the people. And the LORD
> said to Moses, "Make a fiery serpent and set it
> on a pole, and everyone who is bitten, when
> he sees it, shall live." So Moses made a bronze
> serpent and set it on a pole. And if a serpent
> bit anyone, he would look at the bronze
> serpent and live.

Who sent the serpents in judgment on the people?

God sent the serpents.

Leader: Who will judge sin at the end of the age?

God will judge sin at the end of the age.

Leader: Who provided a way for the Israelites to be saved from
the judgment?

God provided a way for the Israelites to be saved from the judgment.

Leader: What did the Israelites have to do to be saved from the
serpents?

The Israelites were to look at the bronze serpent.

Leader: If you were an Israelite suffering from the serpent's
bite, what would you think of God's plan to provide healing for you
through a bronze statue?

(Answers may vary.) It seems likely that many thought this was an absurd plan. How could a statue heal? God's plan might have seemed ridiculous, but those who believed God, and did what He said received healing from the judgment.

Leader: How did Jesus compare Himself, the Son of Man, to the bronze serpent?

Jesus said that the Son of Man must be lifted up and that whoever believes in Him will have eternal life. Just as the Israelites looked at the bronze serpent, having faith and belief that by looking they would be healed by God, we are to look to Jesus in faith for our salvation.

Leader: When Jesus says, "the Son of Man must be lifted up," to what was He referring?

Jesus was lifted up on a cross to die for our sins.

Leader: Without Jesus, how are you like an Israelite, in painful agony from a snake-bite?

Like an Israelite suffering from a deadly snake-bite, I am suffering from the deadly consequences of my sin.

Leader: What does Jesus say that you must do to be saved from the deadly consequences of your sin?

I must believe in Jesus. This means that, like the Israelites, I must, with a repentant heart, in faith trust that God's provision in Jesus is the only thing that can save me from God's judgment for my sin.

Leader: Many people assume that they have to make a serious mistake or do something very bad to deserve God's judgment. They assume that if they do all they can to be reasonably good, God's judgment will not be sent on them. What did Jesus tell Nicodemus about this?

*Jesus told Nicodemus that, "whoever does not believe is condemned already." **All** people will be facing condemnation for their sin unless they believe in Jesus Christ, the Son of God.*

Leader: Reasonably good people who do not believe in Jesus will be condemned, like the weeds we discussed in yesterday's devotion. Yet God did not send Jesus to condemn the world, but to save it. Think about the people you know who do not yet believe in Jesus. Will you tell them the good news?

Prayer

Lord Jesus, I thank You that You willingly came to be be lifted up on the cross to save me from judgment and condemnation. The Gospel, Your good news, seems so strange to many people. Please, Lord, open the eyes of our friends and neighbors who have not yet looked to You for salvation. May they look at You in belief and be saved. Help us to be faithful to share this good news with those who are suffering in their sins.

SATURDAY: JESUS AND ZACCHAEUS

Read Luke 19: 1-10

Leader: What city was Jesus passing through?

Jesus was passing through Jericho.

Leader: What was Zacchaeus's job?

Zacchaeus was a chief tax collector.

Leader: What else do you know about Zacchaeus from this passage?

Zacchaeus was rich. He was short (small in stature).

Leader: What did Jesus tell Zacchaeus when He saw him up in the sycamore tree?

Jesus told him to hurry and come down because Jesus was going to stay at Zacchaeus's house.

Leader: How did Zacchaeus respond to this?

Zacchaeus hurried down and joyfully welcomed Jesus to his home.

Leader: What did the crowd think of this?

The crowd grumbled because they didn't like it that Jesus was staying with a sinner.

Leader: Why did the crowd call Zacchaeus a sinner?

Tax collectors became rich by cheating the people, collecting extra money to keep in addition to the tax.

Leader: What did Zacchaeus have to say about this?

He called Jesus "Lord," and he promised to give half of his goods to the poor. He also promised to return fourfold (times four) whatever he had cheated from someone.

Leader: What does this response from Zacchaeus tell you about his heart attitude?

Zacchaeus was repentant. He was sorry for his sin and wanted to turn away from his sinful life.

Leader: What did Jesus say about Zacchaeus?

Jesus said that salvation had come to Zacchaeus's house and that Zacchaeus was a son of Abraham.

Leader: Zacchaeus was a Jew (son of Abraham), but Jesus meant something else by this. Do you remember when we read that John the Baptist said to the Pharisees, "Don't presume to say to yourselves, 'We have Abraham as our father.' For I tell you that God is able to raise up children for Abraham from these stones!" (Matthew 3:9)? When Jesus told Zacchaeus that salvation had come to his house since he was a son of Abraham, what did Jesus mean?

Jesus meant that Zacchaeus was a true son of Abraham, one of the Kingdom of God.

Leader: Jesus then said something remarkable. What did Jesus say in verse 19?

Jesus said that the Son of Man has come to seek and to save the lost.

Leader: In the Old Testament book of Ezekiel, God told Ezekiel,

> "For thus says the Lord GOD: Behold, I, I
> myself will search for my sheep and will seek

them out. As a shepherd seeks out his flock when he is among his sheep that have been scattered, so will I seek out my sheep, and I will rescue them from all places where they have been scattered on a day of clouds and thick darkness. I myself will be the shepherd of my sheep, and I myself will make them lie down, declares the Lord GOD. I will seek the lost," (Ezekiel 34:11-12, 15-16a)

If you were a Jewish person listening to Jesus say that He was the Son of Man and that He came to seek and to save the lost, what would this mean to you, knowing what Ezekiel had written?

As a Jewish person who knew my Scriptures, I would recognize that Jesus was talking about the prophecy of Ezekiel that God would Himself search for His sheep like a shepherd. God Himself would seek the lost. When Jesus said that the Son of Man would seek the lost, He was clearly saying that He was the Son of Man and that the Son of Man was God Himself.

Leader: Perhaps you've noticed that Jesus repeatedly showed that He is not just a man, but that Jesus is the Son of Man and that the Son of Man is God Himself. Why is it so important that we acknowledge that Jesus is God?

Because Jesus is God, His life, death, and resurrection, which we celebrate at Easter, change everything. If He were only a man, His death and resurrection would not hold any power for us. Instead, Jesus is God, seeking the lost so that He can save them.

Leader: Jesus gave Zaccheus forgiveness and salvation, but then He gave Zaccheus another gift: He stayed with Zaccheus in his home. What does this teach you?

*After we believe in Jesus as our Savior and receive his gift of salvation from judgment, Jesus wants to be with us. Like his fellowship with Zaccheus, Jesus fellowships with us. His Spirit dwells in us. Salvation is more than escape from judgment, it is the gift of **being with** God Himself forever, starting now.*

Prayer

Lord Jesus, You truly are God. Thank You that You came from heaven, that You are the Son of Man, that You came to seek me and to save me. Thank You that we can be with You forever because of Your salvation.

WEEK FIVE: JESUS IS GLORIOUS

MONDAY: I AM

Read John 8:52-59

Leader: The Jews asked Jesus if He was greater than someone. Who was that person?

The Jews asked Jesus if He thought He was greater than Abraham.

Leader: What is glory?

Glory means great honor, praise, splendor and magnificence. When you mom, dad, or teacher praise you for something you've done, they're giving you glory.

Leader: Jesus answered by saying, "If I glorify myself, my glory is nothing." He then told the Jews that there is someone who glorifies Him. Who glorifies Jesus?

The Father, of whom the Jews say, "He is our God." (Verse 54)

Leader: Who was Abraham?

Abraham was the father of the Jewish nation. God called Abraham and commanded him to leave his home town and go to the land that God would give him, the land of Canaan. God promised Abraham that he would be the father of a great nation. God also promised Abraham that all the world would be blessed through him.

Leader: Jesus said that Abraham rejoiced that he would see Jesus' day. What do you think that Jesus meant?

Jesus meant that the blessing that God promised to the world through Abraham was being given in Jesus.

Leader: Jesus said that Abraham saw Jesus' day and was glad. This confused the Jews. What did they say to Jesus about that? (Verse 57)

"You are not yet fifty years old, and have you seen Abraham?"

Leader: Abraham lived over a thousand years before Jesus walked the earth and spoke with the Jews on that particular day. Yet Jesus seemed to suggest that He knew Abraham personally. What did Jesus say in response to the question?

Jesus told them "Truly, truly, I say to you, before Abraham was, I am."

Leader: Jesus' response upset the people so much they tried to stone Him. What was so upsetting about what Jesus said?

Jesus said, "before Abraham was, I am," and this meant that Jesus was in existence long before His birth to Mary, even before the time of Abraham, and continues to be in existence long after Abraham. Jesus was stating that He exists outside of the span of His life on earth. This is obviously an attribute of God, so the people felt that Jesus was blaspheming God. They didn't seem to consider that Jesus' words might be true.

Jesus' statement went further than that, though, and the Jewish people understood His statement to be the name for God, "I AM," that God gave Moses at the burning bush. God told Moses, "I AM WHO I AM," and Jesus was taking this title for Himself. He was telling the people that He is God, not merely a man.

Leader: Why does it matter to you, today, that Jesus is God?

(Answers may vary.) Jesus is eternal. He always is. This means that He knows me even though I was not living at the time that Jesus lived on earth. Because Jesus is God, He has the power and authority to save me. Because Jesus is God, I know that His teaching is true.

Leader: C. S. Lewis famously pointed out the significance of Jesus' statements in his book *Mere Christianity.* Lewis observes that it is foolish for people to say that they accept Jesus as a great moral teacher, but don't accept Jesus' claim to be God. Lewis wrote,

> "That is the one thing we must not say. A man who was merely a man and said the sort of things Jesus said would not be a great moral teacher. He would either be a lunatic -- on the level with the man who says he is a poached egg -- or else he would be the Devil of Hell. You must make your choice. Either this man was, and is, the Son of God: or else a madman or something worse."

Knowing that Jesus is the Son of God, Lewis said, means you fall at His feet and call Him Lord and God.

Prayer

Lord Jesus, please help us to see You clearly and to believe in You. May we live each moment of our days fallen at Your feet, declaring You Lord. Would you help us to confidently and boldly declare the truth about You to others, that they, too, may know You and worship You as Lord of all.

Tuesday: I Am the Bread of Life

Read John 6:25-40

Leader: The people saw Jesus feed about five thousand people with only five loaves of bread and two fish. After Jesus did this, He crossed the Sea of Galilee. The people, realizing that Jesus was gone, came across the lake searching for Jesus. Jesus told them that they were seeking Him not because they saw signs, but because they ate their fill of something. What was it?

Jesus said they were seeking Him because they ate their fill of loaves of bread.

Leader: Jesus told them to not work for the food that perishes, but to work for what?

Jesus said to work for the food that endures to eternal life.

Leader: Who did Jesus say will give them the food that endures to eternal life?

Jesus said that the Son of Man will give it to them.

Leader: The people asked Jesus what they should do to do the works of God. They wanted to know how they could work for food that endures to eternal life rather than work for food that doesn't last. According to Jesus, what should you do to do the works of God?

Jesus said, "This is the work of God, that you believe in him whom he has sent."

Leader: Jesus told them to work for food that does not perish, then He said that the "work" is belief in the one that God has sent. What does that mean?

This means that the only way to "work" for eternal spiritual food is to believe in Jesus Christ, the one that God sent.

Leader: What did the people say that their fathers ate in the wilderness?

They people said that their fathers ate manna in the wilderness.

Leader: Who did Jesus say gives the bread from heaven?

Jesus said that His Father gives the true bread from heaven.

Leader: Jesus explained what the bread of God is in verse 33. What did He say?

Jesus said that the bread of God is He who comes down from heaven and gives life to the world.

Leader: The people replied that they wanted this bread always. Remember that the people talking with Jesus were some of the five thousand who ate the miraculous meal. What do you think they meant when they told Jesus that they wanted the bread of God?

(Answers may vary.) Possibly they were still thinking about physical food that never runs out. The people followed Jesus to the other side of the lake because they wanted to see more miracles. They didn't want Jesus, they wanted the things that they thought Jesus could miraculously give them.

Leader: Jesus was not talking about physical food. What did Jesus tell the people when they said, "Sir, give us this bread always"?

Jesus told them that He is the bread of life. He said that whoever comes to Him shall not be hungry and whoever believes shall not be thirsty.

Leader: What does it mean that Jesus is the bread of life come down from heaven?

God sent Jesus to satisfy their spiritual hunger and thirst. Only in Jesus will they be satisfied.

Leader: What did Jesus say is the will of His Father in verse 40?

Jesus said that the will of His Father is that everyone who looks on the Son and believes in Him should have eternal life and be raised on the last day.

Leader: What does it mean to have eternal life and be raised on the last day?

Eternal life means life after death in heaven with God forever, escaping the eternal wrath of God for sin. Jesus said that on the last day those who have looked to the Son and believed will be raised from the dead.

Leader: Does it change my life now, before I die, to receive the gift of eternal life, or is this just something that will matter after I die?

Eternal life changes me from the moment I look on the Son and believe. Jesus said those who believe will never be hungry or thirsty again. This doesn't mean that we will always have plenty to eat, but that our souls will be satisfied. There is no soul satisfaction, or peace, apart from Christ.

Leader: When Jesus said that they should not work for food that perishes, He didn't mean that they shouldn't earn money to buy food and care for their families. He meant that they shouldn't seek Jesus for the miraculous, but temporary, things that Jesus might give them. Instead, they should look for the eternal food, the Bread of Life, Jesus Christ Himself. Think about your relationship with Jesus Christ. Do you find yourself seeking Him only to ask for physical, temporary things?

(Answers will vary. Help your family to think about ways that we are like the people who ate Jesus' miraculous food. Sometimes we view our relationship with Jesus only as a way to ask for things that we think we need. Talk through your specific situation and encourage your family to think about how Jesus satisfies more than the temporary things that we tend to ask Jesus for.)

Prayer

Almighty God, thank You for sending Jesus, the Bread of Life, that we might have eternal life and be raised on the last day. Thank You that You have provided for our biggest need, the need to be given eternal life. Forgive us for putting temporary desires above our desire for Jesus.

WEDNESDAY: I AM THE GOOD SHEPHERD

Read John 10: 7-18

Leader: Jesus is talking in this passage. What does He say that He is?

Jesus said that He is the door, or gate, of the sheep. He also says that He is the Good Shepherd.

Leader: Jesus said that He did not come to steal and kill and destroy, like a thief and robber. What did He say that He came for?

Jesus said that He came that His sheep, or people, may have abundant life. He also said that He will lay down His life for His sheep.

Leader: Jesus contrasts the good shepherd to a hired hand. What is the difference?

The good shepherd will not abandon the flock at the first sign of danger because the good shepherd owns the sheep. A hired hand will run from danger, leaving the flock exposed to wolves, because the hired hand doesn't own the sheep or care for them. A hired hand cares only for himself.

Leader: Jesus wasn't actually a sheep-herder. This is a metaphor, or picture, that Jesus used to help us understand Him better. Jesus said that He is the Good Shepherd. Those who believe in Jesus Christ are His sheep. What will the Good Shepherd do to protect His flock?

The Good Shepherd will lay down His own life for the sheep.

Leader: What does this mean for you?

This means that Jesus protects you with His life. He died in your place.

Leader: Jesus said He has other sheep that are not of this fold that He must bring into the flock. What could this mean?

The flock of sheep symbolizes all those who believe in Jesus and have been given eternal life. Jesus was speaking to a Jewish audience and when He said there were other sheep to bring into the fold, He was referring to non-Jewish, or Gentile, believers.

Leader: Why do you think Jesus said that He lays down His life, that no one takes it from Him?

Jesus is Lord of all. No one can do anything apart from His authority. No human can take the life of Jesus. The coming events of Jesus' arrest and death were not a surprise to Him. On the contrary, He was in control of all these events and they happened only according to His plan.

Leader: Why is it important to understand that Jesus gave His life and it was not taken from Him against His will?

It is important because Jesus is God and is greater than all humans. Jesus would humble Himself and die on the cross, but even at this low point, all the events were within His control and under His authority. His death was a sacrifice for our sake, just as a shepherd gives his life for his sheep.

Leader: We have seen over and over in our devotions that Jesus repeatedly states that He is God, often by connecting Himself with Old Testament Scripture passages about God. In fact, we already saw an Old Testament passage in our devotions that talked about God being the Shepherd. Do you remember that?

When we read about Zaccheaus, we read this passage from Ezekiel, in which God says that He is the shepherd that will search for His sheep and rescue them.

"For thus says the Lord GOD: Behold, I, I myself will search for my sheep and will seek them out. As a shepherd seeks out his flock when he is among his sheep that have been scattered, so will I seek out my sheep, and I will rescue them from all places where they have been scattered on a day of clouds and thick darkness. I myself will be the shepherd of my sheep, and I myself will make them lie down, declares the Lord GOD. I will seek the lost," (Ezekiel 34:11-12, 15-16a)

Prayer

Lord Jesus, You are the Good Shepherd. Thank You for giving Yourself for our sake. Thank You that when we have believed in You, You are our Good Shepherd, and we are safely in your flock.

Thursday: I Am the Light of the World

Read John 1:1-13; John 8:12; John 12:46

Leader: Who is the Light of the World?

Jesus is the Light of the World.

Leader: Who is the Word?

Jesus is the Word.

Leader: Since Jesus is the Word, He was in the beginning with God. What does this passage tell you about creation?

John 1:3 says that all things were made through Jesus and without Jesus nothing was made.

Leader: Who came to bear witness about the light?

John the Baptist came to bear witness about the light.

Leader: What does the light do to the darkness?

The light shines in the darkness, which has not overcome it (or understood it).

Leader: What happens if you turn on a flashlight in a dark room?

The light enables you to see. Without light, our eyes cannot see anything.

Leader: What does Jesus enable us to see?

Jesus enables us to recognize Him as God so that we can receive Him, believe in His name, and become children of God. (John 1:12)

Leader: Jesus said, "I am the Light of the world. Whoever follows me will not walk in darkness, but will have the Light of life." (John 8:12) What does this teach you about those who do not follow Jesus?

This teaches us that those who do not follow Jesus do not have light that enables them to recognize Jesus and believe in Him. Apart from Christ, people cannot understand truth.

Leader: Light is a metaphor, or word picture, that can mean truth, purity, understanding, righteousness, and sinlessness. What is darkness a metaphor of?

Darkness is a metaphor for lies, ignorance, blindness, and sin.

Leader: Jesus said that following Him means having the Light of life. What does this teach you about walking in darkness?

Walking in darkness is being dead.

Leader: How is it that without Jesus as their Savior people are dead?

Without Jesus as their Savior, people are dead in their sins. They are spiritually dead because of their sin, which deserves the punishment of death, but they are also dead because their souls are deadened to the truth of Jesus Christ. We are not truly alive until Christ saves us.

> As for you, you were dead in your
> transgressions and sins, in which you used to
> live when you followed the ways of this
> world. . . All of us also lived among them at
> one time, gratifying the cravings of our sinful
> nature and following its desires and thoughts.
> Like the rest, we were by nature objects of
> wrath. But because of his great love for us,
> God, who is rich in mercy, made us alive with

Christ even when we were dead in
transgressions—it is by grace you have been
saved. (Ephesians 2:1-2a, 3-5)

Leader: If you have believed in Jesus, you are walking in the
Light of life. How does this change the way you think about your
daily priorities compared to other people who are walking in
darkness?

*(Answers will vary. Lead your family in a specific conversation about the way
they spend their time, the goals they pursue, the relationships they make, and the
way they spend their money and consider if it is different from how those walking
in darkness, apart from Christ, do those things.)*

Leader: What should you do about the fact that there are many
people in your community who are walking in darkness?

*Although you cannot **be** the light for those in darkness, you are commanded to
testify to the Light, just as John the Baptist did. (Lead your family in a discussion
about how they can testify to the Light of Jesus to those in your community.)*

Prayer

Thank You, God, for Your rich mercy and great love which made
us alive in Christ although we were dead in our sins. Thank You for
sending Jesus, the Light of the World. May You help us to testify to
Your light to all those around us.

FRIDAY: I AM THE LIVING WATER

Read John 7:37-39

Leader: What did Jesus say He would give to thirsty people?

Jesus said He would give thirsty people living water.

Leader: Jesus stood and spoke in a loud voice on the last and greatest day of what?

Jesus stood and spoke on the last and greatest day of the feast or festival.

Leader: This was the last and greatest day of the Feast of Tabernacles, or Feast of Booths (see John 7:2). What do you remember about the Feast of Tabernacles, which is also called Feast of Booths, or Sukkot?

God instructed the Israelites to celebrate the Feast of Tabernacles every year. He gave this instruction when the Israelites were at Mt. Sinai getting the Ten Commandments. The feast was to last seven days, with a sacred assembly held on the first day followed by seven days of offerings, finishing on the eighth day with a sacred assembly and another offering. During the feast the people lived in tents to commemorate the forty years that the Israelites spent in the desert living in tents. The feast also was a time to remember that God's presence dwelt with the people in the Tabernacle. Traditionally, Jewish people read the Scriptures and celebrated the Torah (God's Law) during this feast.

Leader: The Jewish people in Jerusalem were in the midst of celebrating this special feast. The prophet Zechariah gave a special prophecy about the Messiah and the Feast of Tabernacles. Listen to these verses from Zechariah 14:8-9, 16:

> On that day living waters shall flow out from Jerusalem, half of them to the eastern sea and half of them to the western sea. It shall continue in summer as in winter. And the LORD will be king over all the earth. On that day the LORD will be one and His name one.
>
> Then everyone who survives of all the nations that have come against Jerusalem shall go up year after year to worship the King, the LORD of hosts, and to keep the Feast of Booths.

This prophecy was fresh in the minds of the Jews celebrating the Feast of Tabernacles in Jerusalem. Knowing this, what did it mean when Jesus spoke in a loud voice and declared that by believing in Him streams of living water will flow out of their hearts?

Jesus was stating that He is the Messiah. His Spirit dwells within the hearts of those who believe in Him. When Jesus came to earth, He was partially fulfilling the prophecy given to Zechariah. Those who put their faith in Jesus Christ receive the Spirit of God and eternal life, symbolized by living water. Their thirst for salvation is quenched.

Leader: Because Jesus came and died for our sins, when we believe in Him we receive the Holy Spirit who dwells within us. How does the Feast of Tabernacles hint at this miracle?

The Feast of Tabernacles celebrates the fact that God lived with, or dwelt with, His people and that He will do that again one day. This will be completely fulfilled when Christ returns, but for now His believers have His Spirit dwelling in them.

Leader: It is an extraordinary thing that Jesus Christ, King of kings, invites us to come to Him, drink, and receive living water. If

You have received this invitation and put your faith in Christ, how will thinking about this amazing truth affect your attitude when you are worshipping in church this coming Sunday?

(Answers will vary. Encourage your family to think about worshipping with enthusiasm this Sunday, praising God for the gift of Jesus!)

Prayer

Almighty God, we praise You and thank You for giving us Your Spirit to dwell in our hearts, making us alive! Thank You for Living Water that quenches our thirst. May we look forward to praising You this Sunday as we worship in church.

SATURDAY: THE TRANSFIGURATION

Read Mark 9:2-13

Leader: Jesus went somewhere with three of His disciples. Where did they go?

Jesus took them up to a high mountain.

Leader: What were the names of the three disciples that Jesus took with Him?

Jesus took Peter, James, and John.

Leader: What happened to Jesus on the high mountain?

Jesus' clothes became radiant and very white, whiter than any bleached white fabric. We call this "transfigured."

Leader: What does the word "transfigured" mean?

"Transfigure" means to change something to make it more beautiful or elevated.

Leader: Who else did Peter, James, and John see?

They saw Elijah and Moses.

Leader: Who was Moses?

Moses was a prophet of God who led Israel out of slavery in Egypt.

Leader: Was Moses still alive when he appeared with Jesus on the mountain?

No. Moses died over a thousand years before.

Leader: Who was Elijah?

Elijah was a prophet of God who revealed God's Word to the people of Israel when the kingdom was divided into two. This was many years after Moses, but many years before Jesus came to earth.

Leader: Was Elijah still alive, walking the earth when he appeared with Jesus on the mountain?

No, God took Elijah up into heaven by a chariot of fire. He was no longer living on earth.

Leader: Since Peter, James, and John witnessed Jesus glowing brightly and Moses and Elijah, how would you describe what was happening on the mountain?

(Answers will vary.) It was as if Jesus peeled back the curtain and gave them a glimpse of eternal life in heaven with Jesus. Moses and Elijah were there with Jesus, no longer living on earth in their earthly bodies, but alive in heaven in their glorious heavenly bodies.

Leader: Moses and Elijah were the greatest prophets that the Jewish people had ever had. How did this event show Peter, James, and John that Jesus was greater than even Moses and Elijah?

God's voice said, "This is my beloved Son; listen to Him." God was showing Peter, James, and John in a very special way that Jesus had the authority of God because He was God.

Leader: The writings of Moses, given by God and called the Law, and the teachings of Elijah and the prophets, also given by God, had great authority to the Jewish people and to Peter, James, and John. They often spoke of "the law and the prophets." Can you describe how this special transfiguration demonstrated what Jesus had already taught them, "Do not think that I have come to abolish the Law or the Prophets; I have not come to abolish them but to fulfill them" (Matthew 5:17)?

This special transfiguration of Jesus, which revealed Jesus' full heavenly glory to Peter, James, and John, showed that He truly did come to fulfill the Law and the Prophets.

Leader: What did Peter want to do?

Peter wanted to build shelters over Jesus, Moses, and Elijah. Peter was so frightened that he didn't really know how to respond.

Leader: The sight vanished and only Jesus remained, in his ordinary humanness, His heavenly glory hidden once again. What did Jesus order the disciples to do?

Jesus ordered them to not tell anyone what they had seen until the Son of Man had risen from the dead.

Leader: Did the disciples understand what it meant that the Son of Man would rise from the dead?

No, they discussed this, trying to figure out what it meant.

Leader: Why does this event matter to us today?

(Answers will vary. Listen to your family's ideas about this and consider together, if they didn't think of it, the truths listed here.) The transfiguration of Jesus teaches us several important truths.

Those who are in the kingdom of God, as were Moses and Elijah, will continue to live, even though they die. The fact that Peter, James, and John saw Moses and Elijah at the same time that they saw the living and glorious Jesus shows us that there is eternal life.

Those who are in the kingdom of God will spend eternity with Jesus, as Moses and Elijah are doing.

Jesus didn't come to toss out the teaching that God gave Moses and Elijah. Instead, Jesus shows us how He is the fulfillment of all that Moses and Elijah wrote about.

Jesus was fully God and fully human.

There is a glorious place somehow and mysteriously outside of our physical and material universe where Jesus and His people exist together in eternity. This reality is now hidden from us. We believe it by faith.

Prayer

Almighty God, when we stop to consider just how glorious You are, we tremble with fear and joy. Thank You for giving us Jesus. Thank You for Your incredible mercy that is given to us through Your beloved Son Jesus.

WEEK SIX: JESUS IS THE ONLY SAVIOR

Monday: Jesus is the Resurrection and the Life

Read John 11:17-44

Leader: Who was dead and in the tomb for four days?

Lazarus was dead and in the tomb four days.

Leader: Whose brother was Lazarus?

Lazarus was Mary's and Martha's brother.

Leader: Where did Mary and Martha and Lazarus live?

Mary and Martha and Lazarus lived in Bethany, about two miles off from Jerusalem.

Leader: When Martha heard that Jesus was coming, she ran out to meet Him. What did she say to Jesus?

Martha said that if Jesus had been there Lazarus would not have died.

Leader: Jesus told Martha that her brother would rise again. Martha believed this, but when did she expect Lazarus to rise again?

Martha expected Lazarus to rise again in the resurrection on the last day.

Leader: Jesus told Martha something very important. What was it?

Jesus told Martha that He is the resurrection and the life. Whoever believes in Jesus, though they die, they will live. He also said that whoever lives and believes in Jesus shall never die.

Leader: This seems a little confusing. What do you think it means?

Jesus Christ is the One who has the power and authority to raise the dead and give the dead life. It is through believing in Jesus that we can experience life after death. When believers die, their physical body dies, but their soul lives eternally with Jesus.

Leader: Jesus asked Martha if she believed this and she replied by telling her Lord what she believed about Him. What did she say?

Martha said that she believed Jesus to be the Christ, the Son of God, who is coming into the world.

Leader: Do you remember what the word "Christ" means?

The word "Christ" comes from the Greek for "anointed one."

Leader: Do you know what the Hebrew word for "anointed one" is?

The Hebrew word for "anointed one" is Messiah.

Leader: How did Jesus feel when He saw Mary and her grief?

Jesus was deeply moved and wept.

Leader: Why do you think that Jesus wept, since He knew that He was about to raise Lazarus from the dead?

(Answers may vary.) Jesus probably expressed His human emotion and sorrow over the death of a friend and the grief of his friends, Mary and Martha. He also may have been moved to tears by the evil of death itself, which came into the world God had made because of sin.

Leader: Do you think that it is okay to weep over the death of a loved one who knows Jesus?

Yes, grief over the death of a loved one does not necessarily mean that we lack faith in Christ or the resurrection. Like Jesus, we can grieve physical death and grieve the effects of sin. We can also grieve the loss of our loved one, knowing that although we will see them again in heaven, we must continue in this life without that person.

Leader: Jesus commanded Lazarus to come out of the tomb. What happened?

Lazarus came out of the tomb with his hands and feet bound in linen strips, his face wrapped in burial cloths.

Leader: Jesus declared that He is the resurrection and the life. How does what happened to Lazarus prove Jesus' words to be true?

Lazarus came out of the tomb alive after being dead for four days. There is no earthly or scientific explanation for this except that the voice of Jesus Christ holds the power of life.

Leader: Did Lazarus do anything to help Jesus raise him back to life?

No, Lazarus lay dead in the tomb. He had no power to choose to come back to life again. When Christ speaks words of life, even the dead are made alive again.

Leader: What does this teach you about your part in being made spiritually alive in Christ. Have you done something to make it happen?

No, Christ alone has the power to make our dead hearts alive again.

Prayer

Lord Jesus, You are the resurrection and the life! You alone have the power to make our spiritually dead hearts alive again. Thank You, Jesus, for bringing me back to life.

TUESDAY: MARY ANOINTS JESUS

Read John 12:1-8

Leader: Where was Jesus in this passage?

Jesus was in Bethany, where Lazarus was.

Leader: How many days before Passover was it?

It was six days before Passover.

Leader: Who served the dinner to Jesus?

Martha served the dinner to Jesus.

Leader: Who else was eating with Jesus?

Lazarus, Mary, Judas Iscariot, and probably all of the other disciples.

Leader: What did Mary do?

Mary took a pound of expensive ointment made from pure nard and anointed the feet of Jesus. She wiped His feet with her hair.

Leader: What do you think was the meaning of this act?

Mary was anointing Jesus with expensive perfumed ointment as an act of worship. She loved Jesus. She had witnessed the fact that Jesus is the resurrection and the life, and she worshipped Him as Christ.

Leader: Why did Judas protest?

Judas felt that Mary's actions were wasteful. He complained that the money could have been used to help the poor, although he actually didn't care about the poor. The text says that Judas was stealing from the disciples' moneybag, and he was greedy.

Leader: Jesus could discern the thoughts of everyone and knew that Judas was dishonest and would betray Him. Did Jesus scold Judas for his greedy dishonesty and tell everyone that Judas was dishonest?

No, Jesus didn't scold Judas or tell the others that he was dishonest.

Leader: What did Jesus tell Judas?

Jesus told him to leave Mary alone and to let her use the ointment for His burial. People will always have the poor to serve, but He would not always be there, in his earthly body, to worship.

Leader: Jesus was already anticipating His coming death. Mary probably didn't fully understand what was coming, but she knew that Jesus was her Lord. Do you know Jesus as your Lord?

(Answers will vary. Give your family an opportunity to express their faith in Christ.)

Leader: What are some ways that you might be extravagant, going above and beyond what seems reasonable, in your worship of Jesus?

(Answers will vary. Try to encourage your family to be specific about acts of worship. Possibilities might be giving an extra offering, serving in an extraordinary way, singing or playing an instrument in a worship church service, or simply serving around the house more cheerfully because of Jesus.)

Prayer

Lord Jesus, You have done great things for us in Your lovingkindness. When we call on You for mercy, You are faithful to give us Your mercy and grace. We want to bring You honor and worship just as Mary did, for You are deserving of our extravagance. May our hearts eagerly give to You that which is most precious to us, as an act of worship.

WEDNESDAY: THE TRIUMPHAL ENTRY

Read Matthew 21:1-11

Leader: What city were Jesus and His disciples approaching?

Jesus and His disciples were approaching Jerusalem and paused at Bethphage by the Mount of Olives.

Leader: What instruction did Jesus give to two of His disciples?

Jesus told them go ahead to the next village and find a donkey tied there, with a colt. Jesus instructed them to tell anyone who asked about it, "The Lord needs them," and then they will send the animals right away.

Leader: Why did this happen this way, according to verses 4 and 5?

This happened to fulfill the prophecy, "Say to the daughter of Zion, 'Behold, your king is coming to you, humble, and mounted on a donkey, on a colt, the foal of a beast of burden.'"

Leader: What did the crowd spread on the road?

The crowd put their cloaks and branches on the road.

Leader: What did the crowd shout?

The crowd shouted (verse 9):

"Hosanna to the Son of David!
Blessed is He who comes in the name of the
Lord!
Hosanna in the highest!"

Leader: The word *hosanna* means "please save!" The crowd's shout came from Psalm 118:25-26a:

Save us, we pray, O LORD!
O LORD, we pray, give us success!
Blessed is he who comes in the name of the
LORD!

The people greeted Jesus with a shout from this psalm, which is a psalm of thanksgiving and praise. The closing section of the psalm, which includes these verses, is a cry for rescue. Why would the people welcome Jesus into Jerusalem with this shout of praise and cry for rescue?

(Answers will vary.) The crowds were welcoming Jesus as one who came in the name of the Lord, bringing salvation and deliverance.

Leader: Who did the crowd say that Jesus was?

The crowd said He was the prophet Jesus, from Nazareth of Galilee.

Leader: What do you think the crowd expected Jesus to do for them?

The crowd probably expected Jesus to save them or rescue them from the Romans who ruled over their homeland. They likely thought that Jesus would rise victorious over the Romans and rule over them with justice, as they interpreted the prophecies to predict.

Leader: Jesus didn't rise to be a ruler or king over the people. Why not?

God knows that our real problem is the sin that will bring judgment on our souls. It is our sin that has broken our relationship with God, making us an enemy of God. We need this relationship repaired, or reconciled. Romans 5:10 says,

For if, when we were enemies, we were
reconciled to God by the death of his Son,

much more, being reconciled, we shall be
saved by his life.

Jesus came to rescue us from our sin and reconcile us to God.

Leader: Why do so many Old Testament passages talk about
the Messiah ruling as a strong and mighty King?

*Jesus will come a second time, bringing judgment and justice. He will one day
reign as the righteous and true King.*

Leader: Throughout this Lenten period, we've discovered over
and over again that we need God's mercy. We've seen that Jesus is the
Son of God and the Son of Man. He is the One with the authority
to forgive sins and heal our broken relationship with God. In today's
passage Jesus entered Jerusalem just days before He would die on the
cross and suffer the judgment that you and I deserve. What would
you say to Jesus as He headed toward His purpose?

*(Answers may vary. Encourage your family to express in their own words
"hosannas" and thanksgiving to Jesus.)*

Prayer

Lord Jesus, we echo the shouts of "Hosanna!" and ask You to
please save us! Hosanna! Blessed is He who comes in the name of
the Lord! May we remember, in the midst of our daily living, that we
need Your rescue and we are grateful for Your sacrifice.

THURSDAY: THE LAST SUPPER

Read Matthew 26:17-30

Leader: What special meal were Jesus' disciples preparing for?

They were preparing for the Passover meal.

Leader: What is the Passover meal?

Passover is a special celebration that God commanded the Jewish people to have every year to remember what God did to deliver the Israelites from slavery in Egypt. After God sent nine plagues on the Egyptians, He sent the final plague, the death of the firstborn. God provided for His people, however, by instructing them to slaughter their best and perfect lamb, brush the blood on their doorposts, and eat the lamb. The Angel of the LORD that struck down all the firstborn in Egypt would pass over the homes that had blood on their doorposts and spare their firstborn.

Leader: Jesus reclined at the table and ate with his twelve disciples. He told his disciples something that greatly saddened them. What was it?

Jesus said that one of them would betray Him.

Leader: Who would betray Jesus?

Jesus said it was the one dipping in the dish at the same time as Jesus did. This was Judas (verse 25).

Leader: Jesus said, "The Son of Man goes as it is written of him." What does this mean?

Jesus meant that the prophets in the Old Testament wrote about the Son of Man dying.

Leader: None of the events of Christ's death was a surprise to God. God is sovereign over all that happened. This means that God was in control of all that happened, and He was like a king reigning supreme over it. Judas was the betrayer, but even without Judas, Christ's death would have still taken place because this was God's design. Does this mean that Judas shouldn't be blamed for what he did?

In verse 24 Jesus said, "But woe to that man by whom the Son of Man is betrayed!" While God is sovereignly ruling over each detail, Judas was still held accountable for his sin in betraying the Son of Man, Jesus Christ.

Leader: Does this teach you something about your own actions and God's sovereign rule over all things?

I am judged for my sin and will be called to account for my actions, even though God is sovereign over all that I do. I can do nothing that God has not known or planned, but I still am responsible for my actions. Scripture is plain that I am free to act (John 3:36), but it is also clear that nothing happens apart from God's will (Romans 9:14-24). (This is a very difficult truth that perplexes thinkers of every age. Encourage your family to trust God and pray for more faith and understanding about God's sovereignty.)

Leader: What did Jesus say about the bread that He blessed and served to His disciples?

Jesus said that it was His body.

Leader: What did Jesus say about the cup that he offered to all of the disciples?

Jesus said that the drink was His blood of the covenant, poured out for the forgiveness of sins.

Leader: The blood of the covenant was a familiar phrase to the disciples. When God gave the Law to Moses, and made a covenant (promise-agreement) with Israel, God instructed Moses to seal the covenant with blood from a sacrifice. Moses sprinkled the people with the blood of the covenant (Exodus 24). What did it mean that Jesus said the drink was His blood of the covenant?

Jesus established a new covenant with His people, this time sealed with His blood. Rather than an animal sacrifice, Jesus was the sacrifice and His blood sealed God's covenant with His people.

Leader: Jesus and His disciples are celebrating Passover, eating lamb in commemoration of the first Passover. Does this remind you of something that John the Baptist said about Jesus?

John the Baptist called Jesus the Lamb of God.

Leader: Why is this so important to you?

God sent Jesus to be the once-and-for-all sacrifice for sins. In the old covenant that God made with Israel, animals were sacrificed to cover the sins of the people. People needed to bring sacrifices repeatedly throughout their lives. Through His Son Jesus, God made a new covenant. Jesus was perfect, without sin, but would bear the punishment of sinners, which is death.

Prayer

Father God, we thank You for making a new covenant in Jesus. May we remember each time we take communion that we are celebrating what You provided for us. May the full significance of the new covenant fill us with thanksgiving and praise for You.

Friday: Jesus Washes the Disciples' Feet

Read John 13:1-11

Leader: What did Jesus do for His disciples in this passage?

He washed their feet.

Leader: What did the disciples gather for?

The disciples gathered for the Passover supper, or the last supper, that we read about yesterday.

Leader: Describe what Jesus did to wash their feet.

Jesus took off His outer garment and tied a towel around His waist. He poured water into a basin, washed their feet, and wiped them dry on the towel.

Leader: What do you think Jesus' posture was?

Jesus had to kneel or crouch down to wash the feet of His disciples.

Leader: Because people in this time walked everywhere in sandals, feet were often dirty. A host would provide for his guests' feet to be washed, but it was a menial task. We don't do this today, but what are some menial service jobs in our culture?

(Answers will vary. Possibilities include house cleaners, hotel maids, office janitors, waiting on tables, etc.)

Leader: Why did Peter object to Jesus washing his feet?

Peter believed that Jesus was his Lord. He didn't think it was right for his Lord to serve him, especially in such a lowly task.

Leader: What was Jesus' reply?

Jesus told Peter than if Jesus didn't wash Peter's feet, Peter would have no part with Jesus.

Leader: How did Peter respond to Jesus?

Peter asked Him to wash not just his feet but his head and hands as well.

Leader: What did Jesus say about Peter's request?

Jesus told Peter that once someone is bathed, he is clean and only needs to wash his feet.

Leader: Did Jesus say that Peter was clean?

Yes, Jesus said that Peter was clean.

Leader: What do you think Jesus meant by this?

Jesus meant Peter had already received salvation, which cleansed his heart from sin, when He said that Peter had already been bathed. The foot-washing symbolized the daily cleansing that a believer receives when they confess their daily sins. I John 1:9 says,

> "If we confess our sins, he is faithful and just
> to forgive us our sins and to cleanse us from all
> unrighteousness."

Leader: If you have put your trust in Jesus Christ and received salvation the Bible teaches that you are justified before God. This means that you are not condemned for your sin. However, the sins that you commit every day stand in the way of your relationship with God. Like the dirt on Peter's feet, these sins need to be washed clean. We need to be forgiven of our daily sins so that our relationship with God is strong.

Prayer

Before I pray aloud, we will have a time of silent prayer. During this time, you can confess your sins to Jesus and thank Him that He has forgiven you.

Lord Jesus, we are saddened that we continue to sin, but we are thankful that You are faithful to wash us and cleanse us from our sins.

SATURDAY: JESUS IS THE WAY, THE TRUTH, AND THE LIFE

Read John 14: 5-11

Leader: This conversation between Jesus and His disciples took place during their last supper. Who asked Jesus how he could know know the way?

Thomas asked Jesus how he could know the way.

Leader: What did Jesus answer?

Verse 6 says, "Jesus said to him, "I am the way, and the truth, and the life. No one comes to the Father except through me"

Leader: Who is the Father?

The Father is God, the eternal Creator God who sent Jesus, His Son.

Leader: Philip asked Jesus to show him the Father. Jesus responded by asking Philip, "Have I been with you so long, and you still do not know me, Philip?" Why did Jesus say that?

Jesus was teaching Philip that Jesus is one with the Father. Jesus is God, He is in the Father and the Father is in Him.

Leader: Jesus said that Philip should believe that Jesus is in the Father and the Father is in Him, or at least believe what?

Jesus said "or else believe on account of the works themselves" (ESV) or "at least believe on the evidence of the miracles themselves." (NIV1984)

Leader: Think over all that we've read during Lent about Jesus. What do you think Jesus meant by saying, "or else believe on account of the works themselves"?

Jesus had repeatedly demonstrated through miracles and fulfilled prophecies the truth that Jesus is in the Father and the Father is in Him. Throughout all His miracles and teachings, Jesus purposefully proved that He is the Son of God and the Son of Man. There should be no question in Philip's mind or in ours about His identity and authority.

Leader: When something is completely true, without dispute, it is called absolute truth. For instance, the fact of gravity is an absolute truth. You might say you don't believe gravity, but if you drop something from your roof, it will fall to the earth no matter what you believe. Gravity is an absolute truth. Absolute truth should be obvious. If something is true it is absolutely true. If it isn't absolutely true, how could it be true at all? However, in our time many people no longer have confidence in absolute truth.

The existence of God is an absolute truth, but many people deny this truth. People are uncomfortable insisting on the truth of *ideas or beliefs* that cannot be proven as easily as gravity. Because of this, they say that your beliefs are "true for you" and that their beliefs are "true for them." This is called relative truth. What would you say is the problem with relative truth?

Two contradictory beliefs cannot both be true.

Leader: Absolute truth seems obvious. Why do you think that people don't feel comfortable with absolute truth?

(Answers will vary.) People don't want to be told that they are wrong. They also don't want to tell others that they are wrong. It is easier to pretend that all ideas are somehow right, even when this is an absurdity.

Leader: What does the word "exclusive" mean?

"Exclusive" means other things or ways are left out and only one thing or way is included. If a store sells a product exclusively, they are the only store that carries the product. If a book focuses exclusively on math, there is nothing in the book related to history or geography or English or any other subject but math.

Leader: Jesus said that He is the way, the truth, and the life. Does this leave room for anyone or anything else to be the way, the truth and the life?

No, if He is the way, the truth, and the life, then no one else can be these things.

Leader: Jesus' second statement, "No one comes to the Father except through me," makes it clear that no one else can be the way, the truth, and the life. Why is this an exclusive statement?

Jesus is the only way to salvation. He excludes all other possibilities for salvation when He said that He is the only way.

Leader: Does Jesus teach absolute truth or relative truth?

Jesus teaches absolute truth.

Leader: Why do you think that some people complain that it is arrogant or prideful for Christians to say that Jesus is the only way to salvation?

(Answers may vary.) Because people do not have confidence in absolute truth, they are unwilling to insist that one thing is true and that the opposite is false. When Christians testify to what Jesus said, Christians are stating that all other beliefs must be false. Rather than considering if that is possible, many people are offended and label Christians as arrogant and prideful.

Leader: Do you think it is prideful to tell others that Jesus is the only way to come to God?

*(Answers may vary. Listen to your family, then re-affirm what Jesus said.) It isn't prideful to testify to truth. We don't say that Jesus is the only way because it is our idea, and we are pushing ourselves on others. We say that Jesus is the only way because it is **true**. We are not arrogant to insist that if you jump out of an airplane you will fall to the earth and die. We insist on that warning because it is **true**. We testify to what is true because it is true, not because it is our idea.*

Prayer

Father God, thank You for giving us a way to come to You. Thank You for Jesus. Forgive us that we sometimes feel uncomfortable standing firm in testifying that Jesus is the way, the truth, and the life. May Your grace give us the conviction to boldly testify that Jesus is the only way to come to God. May You show us how our thinking has become influenced by relativism so that we can repent and think correctly about what is True.

HOLY WEEK: JESUS CHRIST, GOD'S ANOINTED ONE

MONDAY: BETRAYAL IN THE GARDEN

Read Matthew 26:36-56

Leader: What was the name of the place where Jesus went to pray?

The place was called Gethsemane.

Leader: What did Jesus tell His disciples to do while Jesus prayed?

Jesus told them to sit and wait.

Leader: Which disciples did Jesus take with Him?

Jesus took Peter and the two sons of Zebedee.

Leader: How did Jesus feel at that moment?

Jesus was sorrowful and troubled in His soul, overwhelmed to the point of death.

Leader: In His sorrow, what did Jesus do?

He fell on His face and prayed to the Father, asking that if possible the cup would pass from Him, but if not, Jesus wanted the will of God.

Leader: Jesus prayed "My Father, if it be possible, let this cup pass from me." What was the "cup"?

The "cup" was a way of describing the suffering that Jesus would experience by taking the punishment for sin on the cross. He meant both the physical suffering, but more importantly the spiritual suffering of receiving the wrath or anger of God.

Leader: Jesus told the Father that if the cup could not pass, that Jesus wanted the Father's will. Jesus was submitting to the purpose of God the Father. When you pray for God to take away something hard, are you willing to submit to God's purposes for you, even if it means that God will not take away the hard thing?

(Answers will vary.)

Leader: What did the disciples do while Jesus prayed?

The disciples fell asleep while Jesus was praying.

Leader: Jesus saw Judas coming along with a group of armed men, sent from the chief priests and elders of the people. How did Judas greet Jesus?

Judas greeted Jesus with a kiss.

Leader: In Israel in Jesus' day, greeting one another with a kiss was as common as a friendly handshake is today. How did Jesus reply to Judas' greeting?

Jesus told Judas to do what he came to do.

Leader: Peter cut off the ear of the high priest's servant after Jesus was seized and arrested. What did Jesus tell Peter?

Jesus told Peter to put away his sword. Jesus also reminded Peter that Jesus had complete authority and power over all that was happening. Jesus said that at anytime He could call upon twelve legions of angels. Jesus said that all of this must happen to fulfill Scripture.

Leader: Why was Jesus treated like a rebel leader and like a violent threat?

It didn't make any sense that they treated Jesus like a violent rebel, but Jesus explained that it was happening that way to fulfill Scripture.

Leader: Although Peter and all the disciples fled the scene, many years later Peter wrote about this moment. Listen to 1 Peter 2:21-24:

> For to this you have been called, because
> Christ also suffered for you, leaving you an
> example, so that you might follow in his steps.
> He committed no sin, neither was deceit
> found in his mouth. When he was reviled, he
> did not revile in return; when he suffered, he
> did not threaten, but continued entrusting
> himself to him who judges justly. He himself
> bore our sins in his body on the tree, that we
> might die to sin and live to righteousness. By
> his wounds you have been healed.

According to Peter, why did Jesus suffer?

Jesus suffered so that we might die to sin and live to righteousness. Jesus healed us through His suffering. Jesus also gave us an example to follow. After we have been healed from our sin, Jesus makes it possible for us to suffer injustice and submit to sinful authorities with the same trust for God the Father, the just Judge, that Jesus had.

Prayer

Lord Jesus, thank You for suffering for our sake. Thank You that You made it so that we could die to sin and live to righteousness, by Your grace. May we return to You, the Shepherd and Overseer of our souls.

Tuesday: Jesus is Tried by the High Priest

Read Matthew 26:59-68

Leader: What did the chief priests and the whole council want to do to Jesus?

The chief priests and the whole council wanted to put Jesus to death.

Leader: Two men came forward and accused Jesus. What did they accuse Jesus of saying?

The two men accused Jesus of saying, "I am able to destroy the temple of God, and to rebuild it in three days." (Verse 61).

Leader: What did Jesus say in response?

Jesus remained silent.

Leader: The high priest asked Jesus if He was the Christ, the Son of God. What did Jesus say in answer to this question?

Jesus said, "You have said so. But I tell you, from now on you will see the Son of Man seated at the right hand of Power and coming on the clouds of heaven."

Leader: When the high priest heard this, he was shocked and tore his clothes and accused Jesus of blasphemy. Blasphemy is dishonoring God's name. What did the council say would be the penalty for blasphemy?

The council said that Jesus deserved death.

Leader: Was Jesus committing blasphemy?

No, He was not. Jesus is God and was stating the truth. The high priest and the council did not believe that Jesus is God.

Leader: The high priest and the council were high-ranking Jews. They knew the Scriptures. Do you think that they knew God the Father and had faith in Him for their salvation?

No, they did not know God the Father, nor did they have faith in Him. We read in John 14 that Jesus is in the Father and the Father is in Him. If the high priest and the council truly knew God the Father, they would have recognized Jesus.

Leader: Is it possible to know your Bible but not know God and Jesus?

Yes, many people know the Bible well, but do not know God and Jesus.

Leader: While it is possible to know the Bible and not know Jesus, we need to remember that the Bible is the way that God chose to reveal Himself to us. If we want to know God, we need to read and study the Bible. How can we guard against knowing the Bible but not knowing Jesus?

It is important that we pray for the Holy Spirit to open our eyes, that we might be able to know Jesus. It is by God's grace through faith, not by anything that we do, that we know Jesus.

Prayer

Father God, please open our eyes to You. We don't want to be like the high priest and the council, who didn't recognize You when You stood before them. As we read and study Your Word, the Bible, please reveal Yourself to us.

WEDNESDAY: PETER DENIES JESUS

Read Matthew 26:30-35; 26:69-75

Leader: Before Jesus was arrested, Peter promised Jesus something. What was it?

Peter promised that even if everyone else fell away from Jesus, he would not. Peter also promised that he would die with Jesus before he would deny Jesus.

Leader: When Jesus was arrested, what did Peter do?

Peter fled with the others.

Leader: While the high priest was questioning Jesus, Peter was in the courtyard. A servant girl recognized Peter. What did she say to Peter?

The girl said, "You also were with Jesus the Galilean."

Leader: What did Peter say in response?

Peter said he didn't know what she meant. He denied it.

Leader: What did the second servant girl say?

The second servant girl said, "This man was with Jesus of Nazareth."

Leader: What did Peter say in response to this?

Peter denied it with an oath and said, "I do not know the man."

Leader: After a while some bystanders came up to Peter and said that Peter must be one of Jesus' followers because his accent gave him away. What did Peter say in response?

Peter cursed and swore that he did not know Jesus.

Leader: How many times did Peter insist that he didn't know Jesus?

Peter insisted that he didn't know Jesus three times.

Leader: What happened after the third time?

After Peter's third denial, the rooster crowed.

Leader: When Peter heard the rooster crow, what did Peter immediately remember?

Peter heard the rooster crow and immediately remembered that Jesus said he would deny Him three times before the rooster crowed in the morning.

Leader: Peter had faith in Jesus, but under pressure and in fear, he denied knowing Jesus. When Peter heard the rooster and remembered Jesus' words, how did Peter feel?

He wept bitterly. Peter was deeply grieved about what he had done. He was repentant.

Leader: How do you feel when you realize the ugly truth of a sin that you have committed?

(Answers will vary.)

Leader: How is genuine repentance for sin different from regretting a sin?

While repentance is often accompanied by regret, it is possible to regret a sin without being repentant. True repentance flows from a heart attitude that hates sin and loves righteousness. Sometimes sinners regret their sin because of the consequences that they suffer, but not because they hate sin.

Leader: When you get in trouble because of something that you did wrong, do you tend to react with regret or with repentance?

(Answers will vary.)

Leader: How do you think a repentant person will respond when their sin is pointed out to them or they are rebuked for it?

(Answers will vary.) A repentant person might feel upset at first to be rebuked for sin, but ultimately a repentant person is thankful to be rebuked for sin because in their heart they desire to turn away from sin and ask for God's mercy and forgiveness.

Leader: It isn't easy to be thankful when you get in trouble. How can you learn to do this?

(This is a tricky question. Allow a few answers, but then direct your family to this answer.) It is only by God's grace and the power of Christ that we are able to be thankful for rebukes. Our sinful nature does not want anyone to correct us for our sin. With the help of Jesus, we can be thankful for correction and remember that whoever is correcting us, it is actually God working to make us more like Jesus.

Prayer

Almighty God, forgive us for our sin and help us to be truly repentant. Help us to react to rebuke or correction with genuine sorrow for our wrong-doing. Thank you that you love us and stand ready to forgive us, just as you loved Peter and forgave him.

MAUNDY THURSDAY: PILATE

Read John 18:28-19:16

Leader: Early in the morning the Jewish leaders took Jesus to the governor. What was the name of the Roman governor?

The Roman governor's name was Pilate.

Leader: Pilate asked the Jewish leaders why they didn't judge Jesus themselves. What did the Jewish leaders tell Pilate?

The Jewish leaders said it was not lawful for the Jewish leaders to put Jesus to death.

Leader: Did the Jewish leaders want Jesus to be put to death?

Yes, the Jewish leaders wanted Jesus put to death.

Leader: What did Pilate ask Jesus?

Pilate asked Jesus if Jesus was the King of the Jews.

Leader: How did Jesus answer Pilate? (John 18:34)

Jesus asked Pilate if he was asking on his own, or if others had said it about Jesus.

Leader: Pilate said, "Am I a Jew?" Pilate didn't pretend to understand the Jewish laws or traditions. Pilate asked Jesus what Jesus did. How did Jesus reply to this? (John 18:36)

Jesus told Pilate that His kingdom is not of this world.

Leader: Jesus told Pilate that Jesus was born for a specific purpose. What was that purpose?

Jesus was born and come into the world to bear witness to the truth.

Leader: What did Pilate ask Jesus?

Pilate asked Jesus, "What is truth?"

Leader: What did Pilate and his soldiers do to Jesus?

Pilate beat Jesus, or flogged Him, with a whip. Pilate's soldiers mocked Him, put a crown of thorns on His head, dressed Him in a purple robe, called Him "King of the Jews," and slapped Him.

Leader: The chief priests and officers cried out for Jesus to be crucified. They wanted Jesus killed by nailing Him to a cross. The Jews said something to Pilate that frightened Pilate. What frightened Pilate?

The Jews told Pilate that Jesus claimed to be the Son of God, which frightened Pilate.

Leader: Why do you think Pilate was afraid when he heard this?

(Answers may vary.) Pilate was probably afraid because he realized that if Jesus really was the Son of God, then Pilate was opposing God.

Leader: Pilate told Jesus that Pilate had the authority to release Jesus. What did Jesus tell Pilate?

Jesus told Pilate that Pilate would have no authority over Jesus at all unless God gave it to Pilate.

Leader: What was God's purpose in sending in Son Jesus?

God's purpose in sending Jesus was providing for the salvation of sinners. It was God's design and God's will that Jesus die.

Leader: Could Pilate or anyone else kill Jesus if it was not God's design and will?

No, no one could kill Jesus unless it was God's design and will. In fact, in John 8:59 the Jews tried to stone Jesus, but it was not God's plan for Jesus to die at that time, and Jesus slipped away unharmed.

Leader: Why do you think it is important to understand that Jesus' death was God's will?

(Answers will vary.) We need to understand that Jesus' death on the cross was God's plan from the beginning. God, in His mercy, provided a way for sinners to be saved from the punishment for sin.

Leader: When we say that Jesus paid for our sin, freeing us from the punishment of death by dying on the cross in our place, we say that Jesus "redeemed" us. We "owed" the price of death for our sin and by dying in our place, Jesus "paid" that price, freeing us. God's plan to provide for our redemption through Jesus is called God's "redemptive plan." Do you think that God had to send Jesus?

No, God did not have to send Jesus. He did not have to save us from our sin. When Adam and Eve sinned against God, all of humanity was cursed by God for sin. God does not owe us redemption. We don't deserve to be spared from the punishment for sin.

Leader: Can you think of any Bible verses that explain why God sent Jesus to redeem us?

(Answers will vary. Listen to the verses that your family suggests and then share these.)

God sent Jesus to redeem His people because He loves His people.

> For God so loved the world, that he gave his
> only Son, that whoever believes in him should
> not perish but have eternal life. (John 3:16)

God sent Jesus to redeem His people because it shows His people God's glory.

> When Jesus had spoken these words, he lifted
> up his eyes to heaven, and said, "Father, the
> hour has come; glorify your Son that the Son

may glorify you, since you have given him
authority over all flesh, to give eternal life to
all whom you have given him. And this is
eternal life, that they know you the only true
God, and Jesus Christ whom you have sent. I
glorified you on earth, having accomplished
the work that you gave me to do. And now,
Father, glorify me in your own presence with
the glory that I had with you before the world
existed. (John 17:1-5)

Prayer

Father God, we are amazed that You provided for our
redemption through Your Son Jesus. Jesus willingly submitted to
beatings and mockery in my place. Lord God, You alone authorized
Pilate to treat Jesus in that horrible way, and You did this to show us
how glorious and magnificent You are. Thank You, God, for Your
salvation!

GOOD FRIDAY: THE CRUCIFIXION

Read John 19:16-42

Leader: What was the name of the place where Jesus was crucified?

Jesus was crucified in a place called The Place of a Skull, or Golgotha.

Leader: Who was crucified with Jesus?

Two others, one on each side, were crucified with Jesus.

Leader: What inscription did Pilate write and put on the cross?

Pilate wrote, in Aramaic, Latin, and Greek "Jesus of Nazareth, the King of the Jews."

Leader: What did the soldiers do with Jesus' clothes and tunic?

The soldiers divided His clothes but cast lots for His tunic, because they didn't want to ruin it by ripping it apart. Casting lots means that they decided who would get to keep the tunic by lot, sort of like drawing straws.

Leader: Why did the soldiers do this, according to John?

The soldiers divided Jesus' clothes and cast lots for His tunic because the Scriptures prophesied that it would happen. (Verse 24)

Leader: What did the soldiers give Jesus to drink when Jesus said He was thirsty?

The soldiers gave Jesus sour wine.

Leader: What did Jesus say after taking the sour wine?

Jesus said, "It is finished."

Leader: We've been studying Jesus' life and ministry. What was Jesus' purpose in coming into the world?

Jesus' purpose in coming into the world was to provide salvation for sinners. Jesus told Nicodemus in John 3:17,

> For God did not send his Son into the world
> to condemn the world, but in order that the
> world might be saved through him.

Leader: What do you think Jesus meant when He said, "It is finished"?

Jesus meant that He had accomplished what God had sent Him to do. By dying a death that Jesus did not deserve, Jesus was the substitute for sinners and died in the place of sinners.

Leader: Jesus also told Nicodemus in John 3:18,

> Whoever believes in him is not condemned,
> but whoever does not believe is condemned
> already, because he has not believed in the
> name of the only Son of God.

Have you believed in Jesus?

(Answers may vary. Give your family an opportunity to express their faith in Christ, but don't push them to affirm something that doesn't come from their heart.)

Prayer

Lord Jesus, You are the only Son of God. Thank You for dying in our place. Thank You that when we believe in You we are not condemned for our sins. There is nothing that we can do to earn this precious gift of grace. Fill us with belief and please help us in our unbelief, that we might believe.

HOLY SATURDAY: JOY COMES IN THE MORNING

Read Matthew 27:50-51; Hebrews 9:23-28

Leader: What happened in the temple when Jesus died?

When Jesus died, the curtain of the temple was torn in two from top to bottom. The earth shook and rocks split.

Leader: Who tore the curtain of the temple?

God tore the curtain of the temple when Jesus died.

Leader: What is the curtain of the temple?

The curtain of the temple separated the Holy Place, where priests could enter daily, from the Most Holy Place, where God's glory and presence was.

Leader: When God gave the old covenant to Moses and Israel, God designed a way for the people to have their sins covered. One day each year on the Day of Atonement, the high priest entered into God's presence in the Most Holy Place. The high priest sprinkled the Ark of the Covenant with the blood of the sacrifices. This atoned for the sin of the people. According to Hebrews, these rites were a copy of heavenly things. What Most Holy Place did Christ enter, according to Hebrews 9:24?

Christ entered heaven itself, into the presence of God.

Leader: Why did Jesus Christ do this?

Jesus Christ did this to "put away sin by the sacrifice of Himself." (Hebrews 9:26)

Leader: The curtain of the temple separated the people from God's glory and presence. Why did God tear the curtain?

God tore the curtain because the new covenant provided, through Jesus Christ's death on the cross, the perfect sacrifice for sin, once and for all.

Leader: Was the old covenant system of sacrifices necessary after Jesus died on the cross?

No, the old covenant system was no longer necessary.

Leader: Why?

Under the old system, which was copy of heavenly things, the sinful priest entered the Most Holy Place once a year with blood that was not his own. Jesus, the sinless priest offered His own blood and paid for sins once and for all. Through Christ's sacrifice, believers in Him can be with God.

Leader: The author of Hebrews says that Jesus will appear a second time. Why will Jesus return a second time, according to Hebrews 9:28?

Jesus will return to save His people, who are eagerly waiting for Him.

Leader: Are you eagerly waiting for Jesus to come again?

(Answers will vary. Sometimes we struggle to eagerly wait for Jesus to come again. This is especially true for children who lead, by God's grace, happy and contented lives.) After we have received by grace the gift of salvation, we will become more and more eager for Jesus to return as we know Him better. If you don't feel eager for Christ's return, ask God to help you know Him better so that you might look forward eagerly to His return.

Leader: The period of Lent has come to a close. Tomorrow is Easter! I Corinthians 15:17-20 says,

> And if Christ has not been raised, your faith is futile and you are still in your sins. Then those also who have fallen asleep in Christ have perished. If in Christ we have hope in this life only, we are of all people most to be pitied. But in fact Christ has been raised from the dead, the firstfruits of those who have fallen asleep.

Because Jesus Christ rose from the dead, His sacrifice has the power to save us from our sins and give us ultimate victory over death. Believers in Jesus will, like Jesus, be resurrected from the dead. Come quickly, Lord Jesus!

Prayer

Lord Jesus, You are our hope! Thank You for giving us victory over death and opening the way for us to be with You forever. "Weeping may tarry for the night, but joy comes with the morning!"*

(Psalm 30:5b)

✝

Believe in the Lord Jesus, and You Will Be Saved

Putting Your Faith in Christ

We are all sinners.

For all have sinned and fall short of the glory of God. (Romans 3:23)

As it is written: "None is righteous, no, not one; no one understands; no one seeks for God. All have turned aside; together they have become worthless; no one does good, not even one." (Romans 3:10-12)

God judges sin.

For the wages of sin is death, but the free gift of God is eternal life in Christ Jesus our Lord. (Romans 6:23)

Whoever believes in the Son has eternal life; whoever does not obey the Son shall not see life, but the wrath of God remains on him. (John 3:36)

God provides for our salvation.

Thus it is written, that the Christ should suffer and on the third day rise from the dead, and that repentance and forgiveness of sins should be proclaimed in his name to all nations. (Luke 24:46b-47a)

For all have sinned and fall short of the glory of God, and are justified by his grace as a gift, through the redemption that is in Christ Jesus, (Romans 3:23-24)

But when the goodness and loving kindness of God our Savior appeared, he saved us, not because of works done by us in righteousness, but according to his own mercy, by the washing of regeneration and renewal of the Holy Spirit, whom he poured out on us richly through Jesus Christ our Savior, (Titus 3:4-6)

Christ died for our sins in accordance with the Scriptures, that he was buried, that he was raised on the third day in accordance with the Scriptures. (I Corinthians 15:3b-4)

For by grace you have been saved through faith. And this is not your own doing; it is the gift of God, not a result of works, so that no one may boast. (Ephesians 2:8-9)

For God so loved the world, that he gave his only Son, that whoever believes in him should not perish but have eternal life. For God did not send his Son into the world to condemn the world, but in order that the world might be saved through him. Whoever believes in him is not condemned, but whoever does not believe is condemned already, because he has not believed in the name of the only Son of God. (John 3:16-18)

Trusting in Christ

The Scriptures are plain: eternal life, forgiveness of sin, and heaven are gifts given to those who trust in Christ as their Savior. We cannot do anything to earn our own salvation, we can only receive this gift through faith.

If God is stirring in your heart a new faith in Christ, you can express your belief in a prayer similar to this one:

Lord Jesus, I am a sinner and deserve God's punishment for sin, which is death. I believe that You died for my sins and that by believing in You I can be saved. Have mercy on me, Lord Jesus I want to turn away from sin and live a life that honors You.

ACKNOWLEDGMENT

I'm thankful for the generous help of my mother, Shirley Shimer, who edited the text and offered her wisdom and advice. She is truly a woman of God and continues to demonstrate to me what it is to hunger and thirst for righteousness.

ABOUT THE AUTHOR

Amy Edwards is a wife and mother of five. Although she spent several years working a corporate job after receiving her degree from Wheaton College, Amy traded this in for full-time mothering and now spends her days homeschooling her children, teaching Sunday School, and sharing her passion for Bible study however she can. Amy and her husband, Howard, live in Wichita, Kansas with their five children.